The Hungry Home Inspector

Why Some Inspectors are Always Hungry for More, While Others Just Go Hungry.

P. Nathan Thornberry

The Hungry Home Inspector
Why Some Inspectors are Always Hungry for More,
While Others Just Go Hungry.
P. Nathan Thornberry

Residential Warranty Services/The Inspector Services Group
698 Pro Med Lane
Carmel, IN 46032
Inspectorservicesgroup.com

ISBN 978-0-9859866-0-5

Cover design by Danelle Smart
Editing by Petra Ritchie
Bellsouth Tower © 2007 Chris Wage
All other photographs courtesy Freebase.com under license CC-BY

Ordering Information:
Quantity sales. Special discounts are available on quantity purchases by corporations, associations, and others. For details, contact the publisher at the address above.

Orders by U.S. trade bookstores and wholesalers. Please contact RWS: Tel: (800) 544-8156; Fax: (877) 307-7056 or visit inspectorservicesgroup.com

Printed in the United States of America

First Edition July 2012

Table of Contents

This book is dedicated to all of the inspectors who work harder than they have to.

I hope this book helps.

Sincerely,

P. Nathan Thornberry

Chapter 1
Beginnings

I remember two things distinctly from when I was six. The first was a one-time event. I was in my room toward the back right corner of our home in Carmel, Indiana. There was a bunk bed and matching dresser and desk, and on top of the desk there were two items- a RCA black and white television, with its own set of rabbit ear antennae, and a standard brown desk lamp (the kind with a flexible neck like you would buy for your six-year-old).

Having been a ride-along guest on home inspections with my dad, an electrician turned home inspector, I felt very competent in diagnosing the electrical problem I was faced with one day. Sitting alone in my room this fateful afternoon, I was playing the Sega Master System for so long that day turned to dusk, dusk turned to night, and I turned the switch on the back of the lamp but the light didn't come on. I removed the bulb, and checked it out. There may have been a slight rattle, but no significant discoloration, so I started to ascertain what could be going on here. The light bulb may or may not be bad, but I didn't know.

So I proceeded to check the light switch that controlled this outlet, it was on. No problem there, and even if there were a problem with that, my parents would certainly inquire why I needed a screwdriver if I went to get one to fit those two tiny screws above and below the switch. This would, of course, result in my dad resolving the issue, not me, and that was a scenario I was not willing to accept.

So I put the bulb back in the fixture, thinking maybe I did not turn the switch for those "two clicks" that it needs to make before it turns on. I knew I had turned it for at least one click, so if I turn it for one more click and then a second click, the light would turn on if the bulb were good at some point. So I turned it one click...nothing. One more click...nothing again.

So now there's only one other possibility, one other variable, before I could be pretty darn certain that this bulb is, in fact, bad. So I removed the bulb, and inserted my right index finger directly into the socket.

This was the first of many times in the decades to follow that I would feel alternating current flow through a finger or hand, something that hardly bothers me today at the right voltage and amp levels, but something about that first time is just really exciting, you know?

When I got back up off the floor, I quickly checked to make sure my arm was the same color and that it had feeling, and then I picked up the light bulb, walked to the other end of the house where part of the garage had been converted into an office, and told my mom with absolute confidence, "This light bulb has gone bad."

It would take something as significant as electrical shock to make the list of things I remember from such a young age as well as that office. The office consisted of a metal desk with a laminate wood top, a typewriter, and files piled up all around the room. The ASHI Code of Ethics was framed neatly and hung on the wall, and then there was that phone. The phone was a constant presence.

The other thing I remember from when I was six years old was the office and the phone, and the phone rule. It gets answered within three rings, period. Why? *If we didn't answer the phone, a competitor would.*

What I couldn't fully understand and really didn't until much later on is that my parents were NOT home inspectors. That's what they called themselves, sure. That's what they did, of course.

They were not simply home inspectors. They were *business owners.*

They were building systems that they could replicate, over and over again.

The rules weren't for them to follow. They were for everyone else to follow. From the way they answered the phone and took an order, to the inspection format and even the standardized comments: "EOPM W/N @ SE CRNR CS," this was the short code that my dad would write on his field form that would then come back to the home office and my mother would type it out: "Evidence of prior moisture was noted at southeast corner of crawl space." It was the start of a system of short codes and standardized notes that remained in use until the day they began using software that allowed them and all of their inspectors to quickly, efficiently, and accurately begin delivering the inspection reports on site. "On-site" is the modern equivalent of the "typed and bound" report of the 80's, when most inspectors were still handwriting their reports.

As a teenager I began taking orders, typing reports, and even looking up codes in the NEC and other code books. I later became the marketing manager, even handled complaints and performed miscellaneous inspection duties, never a full inspection by any means. After typing around 15,000 inspection reports, booking about as many orders, and handling hundreds of "complaints" (the quotation marks are there on purpose), I've definitely had more customer service and report-writing experience than 99% of inspectors out there and probably dealt with more unusual structural and mechanical situations than most as well. I don't say this to build myself up, but rather to gain credibility. You'd be surprised at how many inspectors truly believe that anyone who isn't walking on a roof or getting in an attic every day has nothing valuable to offer, which couldn't be further from the truth.

My parents have also fired me not once, not twice, but a total of three times. Well, my mom specifically. Overall, a quite unique set of experiences for someone in the home inspection industry.

By the year 2000, I was running a home warranty company and a construction and development company, simultaneously shortly thereafter.

In 2001, after being fired by my mother three times, I was hired again...sort of. Having run Residential Warranty

Services, Inc. successfully, she suggested a product to me for companies like hers to utilize: a 90-Day Warranty.

It was an interesting concept, so we wrote it up and Security Home Inspections (my parent's inspection company) began using it almost immediately. I had no idea at the time that this would be something that would change the home inspection industry forever- but I really knew nothing about the "industry." What I knew came from being in a home inspection business. I grew up around it. I was there when home inspections were incredibly basic and almost everyone doing it was also a contractor of some sort with few exceptions, like my parents. I had been there when they got their first office- a two story, hundred-year-old house built next to the train tracks (now a walking path called "The Monon"- considered beachfront property in Carmel, Indiana!). I was there when they were the first home inspection company, probably throughout the Midwest, to occupy a commercial office space. I was there when they built a 10,000 square foot office building and expanded their reach to every major metro area throughout the state of Indiana. I was there for the company outings, I was there when they bought a fleet of Ford Rangers, I was there when they hired a uniform service, and when they added health benefits and section 125 health savings accounts, and I was there when my mother worked closely with our state legislators to get inspector licensing passed.

While dinner conversation was frequently clouded by talk of when GFCI outlets became a requirement for installation in the basement of new homes and the proper size of an egress window, more often we talked about business matters like hiring a sales rep and how they should be paid or what the next marketing piece would look like.

So when we started offering a 90-Day Warranty with every inspection from Security Home Inspections, it just made sense. I had answered the phones for years and sold people on using the company, I knew what Security Home Inspections was about, and I also knew that they weren't the cheapest or most available by far. They were in high demand, and getting that client to book eight days in advance and ask for an extension on their inspection response instead of calling the next guy in the phone book required much more than saying that you are a "good inspector." Longevity stands for many things- we've been in business for 25 + years, we have over a dozen full-time inspectors, full-time mold and radon staff, the first in the area to offer color digital photographs, an office you can call any time and get a live person...all sorts of things like that. People like to hear those sorts of things, but none of them are compelling reasons to consider *none other* than Security Home Inspections. All people have to do is pick up the phone, call any inspector in town, and they'll hear them something like... we're "certified" inspectors, we do a "thorough" inspection, we offer a color digital photo page with every report, etc. With the 90-Day Warranty, there was suddenly a dilemma the other inspectors couldn't handle, because their level of service and

P. Nathan Thornberry

product offerings had never really been called into question. The client would call, ask if they offered a warranty, and the responses would do nothing but convince the client even more that they should go with Security Home Inspections. A few of my favorite responses;

"No we don't."

"That's not a part of our [minimum] inspection standards per [fill in name of organization here]."

"I can't tell you anything about what will happen to the house in the future, I'm just there to inspect."

"But we're cheaper."

It was one of Security Home Inspections' best growth years ever- not only by volume, but also by inspection revenue as well. Prices were increased that year, and the total number of inspection appointments went over 7,000. Their market share was around 22%. In a marketplace with about 80 other licensed firms...you do the math.

It wasn't long before other inspectors were inquiring about the warranties, and that was when I got my first taste of the real world, so to speak. An inspector would call, ask me some questions, figure out I knew what I was talking about, and since at the time I was dealing mostly with local people, I would offer to meet at their office, except they didn't have one. (I didn't think of having them come to meet me at my office until I wrote this book!)

This was mind blowing to me. How can you have a business and not have a business address? The more I learned, the more I was convinced that my parents' business was quite exceptional. Most inspectors don't have an office staff, don't have multiple inspectors, don't have marketing reps. They wish they could afford health insurance but it's nearly impossible without a group plan.

As it turns out, Security Home Inspections was uniquely situated at the front of the herd and had become about the 5th largest single location inspection company in the country, and by far the largest in the Midwest. It wouldn't be until much later that I'd become acquainted with the other top inspection companies and you'll be surprised as you read on about how simple it is to be successful in this business, and how much other inspectors will help you along the way (unintentionally, of course!).

Now, before we go much further, I want to make sure to make some things perfectly clear;

1. There's nothing wrong with small! In fact, there are a lot of great things about it, and there's a whole chapter to cover this, so don't be turned off if you don't want to be that 5+ inspector firm because that is NOT what this book is about.
2. This is not a sales pitch. For those who know me, they know I work with a lot of home inspectors. I

work with mostly successful home inspectors, as the unsuccessful ones or the ones with the unsuccessful mindset won't ever consider even looking at many of our products like RecallChek, 90-Day Warranties, or The Alarm Leads Program. Trying to sell you stuff in a book would not only be lame, but it would be ineffective. I'd rather make you more successful and give you that successful mindset. Then if and when *you* ultimately make the decision to work with us on some level, it will be because you decided to and because it was a good business decision, *not* because you were "sold" something.

3. There are many ways to accomplish the same thing. Spin was invented for a reason, and when I say "spin," I mean the kind of spin that cable news channels put on political issues. Spin should absolutely be used in the way you sell yourself. You should always be confident and *know* you have the best product. Here's a great example: some inspectors deliver reports on-site, others the next day. You can give clients the sense that convenience is key, and that you're good enough and have the systems necessary to deliver the report on site where others fall short. Or you could promote the virtues of reviewing the report thoroughly to make sure the client is taken care of by releasing the report the next day. Either way works pretty well when executed properly.

4. *Nothing* in this book negates the need for knowledgeable and ethical home inspectors. In all

my travels, meeting and speaking to literally thousands of inspectors, it never ceases to amaze me how many believe that good marketing equals haphazard inspections. A few stubborn, unfortunate, self-sabotaging individuals will likely read into this book something nefarious that they conjured up themselves. I am of the opinion that 99% of inspectors out there are really good people and well-intentioned, and most of them do a great inspection. Show me an inspector pointing to another and saying, "That guy doesn't focus on quality like I do!" and I'll show you an inspector who is either A.) Lying to himself, B.) Getting his butt kicked and not making the money he wants (or needs) to make, or C.) Both.

So let's just clear the air right now. I don't know a single home inspector in North America who wakes up in the morning, puts on his uniform, steps out onto his porch and thinks to himself, "You know, today I aim to provide poor service, perform my duties unethically, and miss as many defects as possible." Sounds silly doesn't it? It's the myth of the "bad" inspector and he's just as real as Bigfoot, the Lockness Monster, and the Boogie Man.

Many inspectors pride themselves on doing a thorough job, not realizing somehow that just about everybody in this business has the same level of pride in their own inspections. There are levels of anality, but at the end of the day inspection reports differ mostly in our own minds. (Yes, "anality" is a word.)

They (the inspectors that focus only on quality) put out fliers and business cards that say, "I'm a good home inspector," and then proceed to list all the home systems they inspect, which was a novel concept in the late 70's and even through the 80's, when agents and buyers alike really didn't know what a home inspection was.

Then there are the other home inspectors, the ones that ignore their competition, create a message that can be understood and appreciated by home buyers and agents alike, and they give clients tangible reasons to choose them. You can't turn around without seeing their message. They have logo-ridden trucks and business cards with content on both sides. You can find them weekly at sales meetings talking to agents, delivering fliers and other marketing material. When you call them, they answer the phone consistently and when you ask them why someone should get a home inspection with them, they give you an answer, an actual answer. What you won't hear them say is "because we do a thorough inspection." (The actual answer is the central focus of this book.)

It's the difference between being hungry for more and just being hungry, and that is what this book is about. Open your mind, sit back, and enjoy the journey, because we're going to question everything. By the end, you'll be eating steak every night and hopefully you'll still be *hungry* for more!

Chapter 2
The Journey

It's tough to get a sense of what's going on somewhere without actually being there yourself. You'd think that everyone in Nashville wears a cowboy hat and boots and loves country music if you watched the Country Music Awards on CMT and if country wasn't your thing, you'd have no interest in going. You'd be surprised to know, if you had spent as much time there as I have, that downtown Nashville is quite stunning. Walking between the skyscrapers, on rolling hills of concrete and grates, there are phenomenal restaurants and clubs. There's a B.B. King restaurant with live blues every night. There's a Coyote Ugly- that place where the bartenders dance on the bar every 15 minutes or so and yes, it's the same Coyote Ugly featured in that movie, just a different location. $20 to do a body shot off a bartender, so I hear.

They have a huge music venue downtown, across Broadway from an incredible convention center connected to a ridiculously lavish (and big) hotel. Two of the new skyscrapers downtown, built in the last decade, are high-end condominiums with a style that seems very Chicago or even Manhattan. The only country music related stuff I see when I'm down there is along one strip of Broadway- 9 or 10 bars with live music and a couple of discount boot and hat stores mixed in.

If you've experienced downtown Nashville, you know what I'm talking about. If you haven't, then you don't. You may think it's just a bunch of rednecks listening to [fill in country music star of your choosing here] and running amuck in pickups. You may have a different idea of what it's like, but no matter what that idea is, it won't truly match reality until you go there.

Much the same can be said about success.

Which is why we are starting this book with a journey- the journey I took over the last three decades but mostly in the last ten years- because I could tell you in less than five pages of text exactly what you need to do to be successful in the home inspection business. If we were face to face, it might take less than three minutes. Most of it would have nothing at all to do with any of my products or services. I *could* do that...

BUT THAT WON'T WORK.

It's been proven time and time again. I attended an event in North Carolina, the NCLHIA (North Carolina Licensed Home Inspector Association), and it was a great experience. I probably picked up no less than 45 new clients, which is slightly higher than my usual percentage based on the number of people there. Why was it higher? I had been invited to speak the day before the event, along with Dominic Maricic, Dan Huber, and a few others. Those in attendance listened to great presentations, and accounted for the majority of our signups that weekend. The other inspectors didn't sign up at nearly the same frequency.

There was one moment that was the "proof" I speak of above- the proof that simply giving you the short answers to increasing your revenue levels and overall client satisfaction won't work- and I have a witness to this. A home inspector came up to my booth and started talking to me. He wasn't doing a lot of inspections, he felt real estate agents were in the way and he wanted to go around them (a topic we will cover at length later on, but needless to say...he was wrong!) He was looking for some advice on how to do that. Dan Huber, the witness, looked on with curiosity as I proceeded to tell this particular inspector about how agents in his area largely weren't the problem, but that in fact, he was. He was real estate transaction Kryptonite- for several reasons. Not because he did a "thorough" inspection, not because of what he found or didn't find on his inspections, but because of the way he worded defects and his overall attitude toward agents. Some things he mentioned in his report weren't defects at all.

What inspectors don't realize when they approach the vendor hall at these conventions with trepidation is that most of the vendors there are seasoned professionals who have been around the business as long as or longer than most of the inspectors. As I'm writing this book, we (The Inspector Services Group and Residential Warranty Services, Inc.) are involved in more real estate transactions in a month than the average home inspector could accomplish in over 200 years in the business. That's not an exaggeration. If anything, I'm underestimating for believability.

My point being, you can get some great advice (probably the best advice you'll ever get) from vendors and you'll be surprised at how many vendors don't really "sell" anything at these events. Most are well-established in the industry, and many of them will tell you that the reason they go to events is to keep connected to their clients and deliver support for their products.

At that event in North Carolina, the inspector I was talking to had some serious foundational issues related to his business and I wanted to help him fix that. He didn't want to hear it, he wanted a quick fix and to move on. I helped him as much as I could, then helped him with the "moving on" part and told him to come back and see me in a year or so when his way still isn't working and when he's ready to try it another way. I don't need (or want) someone out there attached to our brand who is hateful or holds disdain for those who refer most all of the inspections that ever happen (real estate agents) and shows it in everything he does.

A month later, he decided to open up and try it "the other way." It worked out great, but he had to take that journey to discover why he needed to change and how he was going to do it without losing his identity. You have to be yourself, just not the self that sabotages your own business and seemingly *hates* money. *My editor who works full time for a major business and finance publication had crossed out the phrase "hates money" and indicated I should change it because in her words, "No one hates money!" Then I had her read two pages of an inspector forum online and she later admitted, "Apparently, there are people who hate money."*

I'm hoping your journey is just a few pages in a book rather than another month of lackluster sales and struggles.

So let's start that journey together, and I'm going to go back several years. Remember at this point that I've been around the business; I think I know everything about it, and I get a call from a friend of my family. He used to run a large inspection company and was in a mastermind group where a dozen of the largest inspection companies in North America exchanged thoughts and ideas with my parents for years (maybe decades) and was running a coaching group now.

As you can imagine, I'm pretty skeptical at this point. If I hadn't known this man for many years, I would have hung up the phone within ten seconds of hearing the word "coaching."

His name is Mike Crow, and he invited me to one of his mastermind groups, this one being held in California.

I wasn't told what to expect, I wasn't told to bring anything, just to show up.

I had no idea walking into that room that by the time I walked out, I would develop lifelong friendships, all home inspection company owners from around the country. We spent three days locked in a conference room of a hotel, talking about all sorts of things. Much of it is proprietary and confidential and I can't share it, but some of it is common-sense marketing stuff we should all be doing and just need a reminder of at times. Mike regularly shares a lot of these things on the public stage.

It was brought to my attention at that meeting by a few of the attendees that there was a huge void in the market. They had heard of my one-year home warranties I sold through real estate agents, knew I did 90-Day Home Inspection Warranties for my parents' company, and wondered if I could do these warranties for them as well.

My response: "Sure, let me look into it."

Usually, I respond with a very quick "YES!" when someone wants to pay for my services, but in this case there were a lot of variables I had to deal with. Various state regulatory issues were the biggest things on my mind. What the attendees in that room didn't know at the time was that the other players in the 90-Day Warranty market weren't just disappointing them on the service and marketing side, they were about to be hit with notifications from multiple states (i.e., Florida, Wisconsin, and The Commonwealth of Virginia) regarding their lack of compliance with those states' laws. What it came down to was that they had no idea these regulations existed because they weren't professionals from the warranty industry. They didn't even have insurance backgrounds. One of the players was super-strong in home inspection, the other was a small venture firm whose largest undertaking appeared to be bison farming. There's only a slight difference between running an agricultural operation and managing risk. In risk management you have to create actuarial models, develop processes, and most importantly, comply with regulations.

A few months later, we had released the RWS 90-Day Inspector Warranty Program nationwide. We started calling, e-mailing, and mailing promotions to home inspection companies. We booked conferences, hired a manager for the operation, and for about four months or so the business was pretty easy to run. The first 300 inspectors or so were easy, they "got it."

"You want to offer a warranty with your home inspections?"

"Yes! That would be awesome!"

And it was awesome. We helped this first group of clients with scripting, customized brochures, and getting the word out. They were using the 90-Day Warranty to separate themselves from the competition in a very real way. They offered a warranty, the competition didn't.

A majority of these companies were multi-inspector firms, the kind I grew up around. They had systems in place, they marketed constantly, and they understood how to inspect thoroughly, the way they had all been taught when they got into the business. At the same time they respected the position they had in the real estate transaction, and respected the "customer" in the transaction (the real estate agent).

This is probably the most difficult concept for most inspectors to grasp: the real estate agent as a *customer*. There's often confusion about who is a *client* and who is a *customer*.

The key difference is this: Without clients, you're not doing any business, and the way to obtain clients is to have a line of customers ready to supply you with business.

This is kind of a difficult thing to do when you have no respect for those who have the potential to make you or break you. There's an entire chapter in this book about how Web pioneers get slaughtered. The chapter isn't what you probably think, I'm not *against* good Web marketing. You should have a good Web site, you can buy ads and do some SEO (Search Engine Optimization), and you can do some consumer direct marketing to supplement your business. The key word being "supplement."

We very quickly ran out of inspectors who ran their businesses professionally and competitively, or at least on the level that they could grasp the concepts we were promoting easily. It became increasingly difficult to convert inspectors into clients and we had to make a change.

The realization had set in...

I (we) knew nothing of the home inspection industry. It was not full of business owners. It was full of home inspectors.

Chapter 3
The Technician Mindset

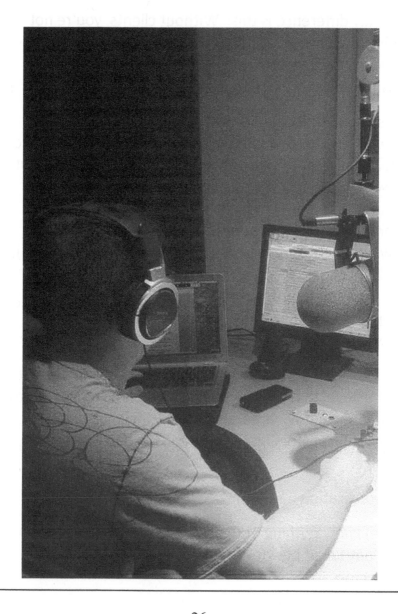

In the spring of 2012, on my weekly radio show on FOX, I had an author by the name of Micheal E. Gerber as a guest. We had an hour-long chat about the *Technician Mindset*. Michael is a big deal, like a *really* big deal. With seven million + books sold, every major business magazine has given him huge credit for his advice to small business owners, and he's been a New York Times best-selling author many times over.

Micheal's book series, *The E-Myth*, is all about the "Entrepreneurial Myth." I highly recommend reading the book, because although it's written for a general audience, it may as well have "Home Inspector" stamped on the front cover.

We are, with notable exceptions of course, an industry full of technicians that are in business for themselves. Most inspectors are operating as a one-man shop, working every day to get orders next week in order to go out, do some inspections, make some money, and repeat the process. The fact that the clients make the checks out to us and the fact that we don't have health insurance, a retirement plan, or regular work hours and paid vacations is what defines many inspectors as entrepreneurs. You can add to that liability that many in the industry have little protection themselves personally from liabilities, both financial and legal, that the "company" incurs.

Why is it that the home inspection industry seems to be so fragmented? Why is it that the average home inspection *company* performs only about 200 inspections annually, with a *gross* revenue of less than $60,000?

More importantly, why is it that most inspectors don't want to do 1,000 inspections or more per year? Why is it that home inspectors don't want to make more than $60,000 per year?

I've tested this theory out more than a dozen times. The first time was at an ASHI chapter meeting. I had an inspector, Tony Smith, a client of mine from Iowa, come up to my booth and start talking to me about how great business was. He asked if I had anything more to offer him in the way of marketing advice, and wondered why I wasn't speaking at the event. I said, "Tony, if you ask any inspector in this room what the most important thing is in their business, I'd say making money wouldn't even make it to the top ten."

He said, "You're wrong! Everybody knows that profitability is the most important thing to running a business, without it you don't have a business!"

I pulled up Microsoft Word on my projector and said, "Okay, let's give this a shot."

It was a break, inspectors were grabbing donuts and coffee, and they were walking up. Tony stood there as I asked ten inspectors in a row what the most important thing to them was in their business.

The first one came up and said, "I would say being very well-educated about home systems."

I typed it up on the screen, agreed, and commended him on his principles.

Tony said as the first guy walked away, "Well, that's just one..."

Next inspector walked up...same question. The response was basically "doing a thorough inspection". Then another inspector said "liability." Then another said "being respected by my peers."

Seven more inspectors came by, gave similar answers, and we kept a list. I saw an inspector I knew who had a multi-inspector firm and I waved him over, asked the same question, and he said without hesitation, "Duh! Making money!"

It was number 11 on the list. Tony's eyes were wide open, and he shook his head as we had another conversation about how inspectors would generally rather hear mechanical theory on how a toilet flushes than anything that makes them look like an actual business that markets to those evil, evil...Real Estate Agents!

So you really think you want to make more than $60,000 per year? Is that so?

Well, how many *pure* business books did you read last year? How many marketing seminars did you attend? How many times in the last year have you gone to a real estate agent, the source of almost all referrals for home inspections, and asked them what would make the home inspection process better or easier?

Maybe I'm being hard on you for no reason. Maybe you do all these things.

Most inspectors do just that: they inspect. They inspect, and then they go home, and then they put together their reports. They send out their reports. They take very good care of their clients...and there's nothing wrong with that, it's just a misnomer to call it "being in business for yourself" if you don't have systems that make it easy, systems that make the process repeatable and duplicable, and a platform that could be run by anyone else with the skill set of a typical home inspector.

Let me give you some examples of the *Technician Mindset*.

- "I'm the only one who can do my kind of inspection."

- "I don't offer clients anything other than a good inspection."

- "I work for the client, and I don't market to those agents. They're not my client."

I could go on and on...but why do that when we can tear these examples apart!

"I'm the only one who can..." Stop! Why would you ever create a process that only *you* could do? Is there any better way to guarantee you'll retire with exactly the amount of money you have in the bank at that time?

The fact is, whether you are planning on making good money and taking vacations and giving yourself a break from doing two or three inspections a day by some point in your 50's, or if you're planning on taking it easy from the start and don't have any inclination to manage people, either way there is no reason to create a process "only you" could do.

This is classic technician mindset combined with mistaking yourself for an entrepreneur when you're really an *inventor* or an innovator or both. I know this disease well, because even though my dad is incredibly business-minded, creates systems and has more than a dozen inspectors and probably 20+ employees at any given time, he's still a technician and an inventor at heart. If it weren't for my mother, the inspection process would be complex and convoluted.

Remember when infrared cameras first hit the scene, and the only available ones cost over $20,000? Yep, my dad bought two and he'd play with them. He gave one to another *inventive technician* who worked for him for more than 20 years, he took it home and started shooting everything in the house figuring out long before any of these IR training companies came around what all they could do with this new technology.

If you've ever seen something on TV or in *Popular Mechanics* and thought to yourself, "I invented that years ago!" – you're prone to making processes complicated. Recognize this; recognize that it is not a strength unfettered. By the way, if you subscribe to *Popular Mechanics* you fit the bill whether you've seen one of your inventions in there or not.

"I don't offer clients anything other than a good inspection." You'll hear it soon enough if you haven't said it yourself. The sad part is that this isn't just something they say to make themselves look "ethical," this is their entire marketing plan.

The *everything else* inferred in the statement is one of two things;

1. Ancillary Services

2. USP's (Unique Selling Propositions)

The ancillary services they don't offer might include termite, radon, water testing, well and septic inspection, pool, spa, etc.

Inspectors who avoid doing these services generally do so thinking they are somehow a more "pure" inspector. "I don't inspect pools because I'm not a pool guy." "I don't check for termites because I'm not a termite guy." Basically I'm an inspector and that's it. My abilities and desire to make money are both equally limited.

What's worse is that inspectors will actually avoid these easy moneymakers like the plague while they dive head first into the deep end of infrared cameras and even energy audits.

It can't be rationalized, so don't try to figure it out. Why would anyone *not* want to be the guy who offers pool inspections? More money, bigger houses...by the way, probably the easiest part of the inspection. But that's how they run their business, not as a business at all.

The USP's (Unique Selling Propositions) are things like guarantees, warranties, checking for recalls with RecallChek, offering agents marketing tools, giving clients discount coupons and rebates on products and services they'll need as a new homeowner. Many inspectors with the technician mindset like to call these things "gimmicks," and when you hear this from an inspector you can be sure of two things.

- This inspector is on the low end of the income range for home inspection company owners.

- He's getting his butt kicked by one of his competitors offering something "gimmicky" and resents the way the world is headed.

He longs for the good old days when putting your number in the phone book and your name on a Website and your business card on the corkboard at Home Depot got you enough calls from people who didn't know who to call that you could make a living. It's sad.

"I work for the client...not the agent!" This is the one where you have to read between the lines and hear the real message. "I don't market."

All inspectors realize, and rightfully so, that yes, we have a responsibility to the client. So whom are you talking to? Whom are you trying to convince of what?

Your obligation to the home buyer or client isn't unique to you at all. You're really just driving home the point that you don't care for real estate agents. You probably think they don't care for you either.

You're probably right. So let's fix it.

Chapter 4
Inconvenient Truths

It's inconvenient that most people need a mortgage. It's built into our system now, no turning back.

Oh, wait! It's a great thing that the home mortgage exists! If we didn't have mortgages, where would we be? A lot smaller houses, that's for sure...and probably far fewer of them.

Even with mortgages that had huge down payments and were done locally and had five-year balloon payments, the world was very different. Take 20% of the mortgage ability off the top and we're back to the days when grandma lived in the den and the kids stayed home until they married.

It's an inconvenient truth that mortgages exist because of the regulations that come with them. Appraisals are a nightmare today. Approvals can be yanked at the last moment and our bank-owned real estate inventory is truly problematic for our country.

They're also inconvenient for real estate agents.

Mortgage guidelines, federal regulations, and the Real Estate Settlement Procedures Act make the agent's job very defined, frustratingly so.

They represent their client, whether it be a buyer or a seller. It's a tough situation to deal with when you have a buyer who's made an offer on the property, it was accepted, and then the appraisal comes in low. What happens now? They have to try to argue with the appraiser, make their case for the value to someone who thinks they know a lot more than the agent does. Or they have to convince the buyer to come up with more cash, or they have to convince the seller to accept a lower price, or a combination of the two.

But that's the sandbox they have to play in. No real estate agent or company or organization thinks that they invented the process. They can add their nuances, maybe some USP's, but they've learned to adapt the process to the mortgages that nearly every transaction is tied to.

For as much criticism of real estate agents as there is from home inspectors, the *inconvenient truth* this chapter is focused on is that many home inspectors have a bigger sense of entitlement than agents do.

It's true.

How many times have you heard a group of inspectors talking about the home inspection process and how it relates to the purchase agreement (or "purchase contract")?

Never.

Successful home inspectors realize that the real estate transaction, the agents, and the purchase agreement are their best friends, even if they're a necessary evil. I've actually always liked the agents I deal with, but I can certainly see why inspectors might not take the same view at all times.

Think of it this way: the real estate transaction is a small island, and while it's in progress the inhabitants are you, the agents, the sellers, and the buyers. Tropical Storm "Mortgage Approval" is heading west towards your position and it's picking up speed as it's hitting warm water full of objections, appraisal issues, and inspection problems...luckily we have this Hurricane Shelter called the Purchase Agreement, cool heads, cooperation, and...uh oh. The inspector just lit the Hurricane Shelter on fire.

Many inspectors will not appreciate the severity of my analogy. They'll say that they're not a part of the real estate transaction. This is coincidentally exactly what most agents in their market probably say about them as well. We found common ground!

There are many inspectors who believe that their job is completely separate from the real estate transaction. I'm convinced that some of them may even believe they invented the inspection process.

What they fail to realize is that the inspection is *defined* in the purchase agreement. No ifs, ands, or buts about it.

Do yourself a *huge* favor and get a blank purchase agreement from your local real estate board. If they won't help you, talk to an agent. Somehow, get your hands on one. I don't care if you have to make an offer on a house, do it. (I would suggest a low ball offer that will not get accepted unless you actually are in need of a house at the moment.)

Find the section regarding the inspection response. Read it.

What did it say?

Did it say anything about the buyer being able to ask the seller to replace something that is perfectly operational simply because it is old?

No!

Let's think about this one for a second. In an earlier chapter, I mentioned an inspector who was "Real Estate Agent Kryptonite." I told you he had some foundational issues in his business, and the way he was reporting some things were creating problems. He said agents didn't like him, which didn't surprise me at all.

You see, he had either no knowledge or no respect for the real estate transaction. Forget the agents for the moment; let's talk about the client, the one we're all obligated to.

The client signed a contract to purchase the property- and within that contract, very clearly defined, was the timing for and subject matter that could be contained within an inspection response. It also had a completely, totally separate section that discussed operational but older appliances and components. It was the section about home warranties.

Thirty years ago, inspectors were largely defining the home inspection industry as it was still in its infancy. The standards varied enormously from company to company, and a large contingency of home inspectors became accustomed to making statements about older equipment suggesting that they were "defunct" or in need of replacement or "beyond their useful life expectancy." Even twenty years ago, there was certainly a place for this tactic when it came to furnaces, air conditioners, and water heaters, but not today. Old water heaters are addressed in the purchase agreement and don't require any predictive statements from the home inspector.

It's not a point that's up for debate; it's a fact that is in writing in a legal document in every real estate transaction throughout the U.S. and Canada.

This rule does NOT apply to roof coverings, as an example. A roof that is gone is gone, whether it's leaking or not. Call it. The rule only applies to mechanical items that fall under extended warranties available to home buyers.

But who are you to say when a water heater needs to be replaced? If it's old, find an issue with it. Run it a little extra, see if you can get it to go lukewarm or cold. Call any actual defect on it you can, but don't try to define the home inspection as something distinct and separate from the defined process outlined in the purchase agreement. If you try to do so, you will succeed, and you won't be a part of the real estate transaction.

If you had presented these facts to as many inspectors as I have, you would know that there will be a guy who stands up and makes a statement that goes something like this:

"I'm not going to do a walk-through inspection for cheap so that I can get business from agents. If they want someone to gloss over defects they can hire someone else!"

It makes me want to ask if they have a hearing problem, or just simply don't understand English.

Who said gloss over defects? Who said walk-through inspection? Who said *cheap*?

Nobody did.

When an inspector has defined his position as being *against* real estate agents he has also defined his business as being non-conducive to the real estate transaction, and that is why he does fewer inspections than he should. That's why he doesn't make as much money as he should.

It's much easier to be thorough when you're prepared to be hated for being so. Being thorough and respected for it is much more difficult, and some inspectors just aren't up to the task, *it's scary to them*. It takes finesse and a little bit of salesmanship.

Chapter 5
The Myth of the Bad Inspector

In late 2010, and we launched a new feature for *RecallChek*. Today it's the most utilized e-mail marketing platform in the real estate industry, and basically, without telling you too much, it's a feature where the client is automatically enrolled in an on-going e-mail campaign with his real estate agent getting the credit. The agent's name goes at the top of the newsletter, the inspector's name to the bottom, with a "Monthly Maintenance Minute" and it's all done for you. It's easy, which is a big part of why it's been a huge success.

As we do with many features, we launched the concept via Webinar. This allows us to get instant feedback from clients and prospective clients, and the Webinar environment allows us to hear objections from inspectors. It prepares us to talk to other inspectors. It costs around $500 per month just to have this service available, but I'd pay $5,000. Don't tell Citrix that please.

I don't remember every Webinar I've ever done, but this one I remember very well.

I was explaining the new feature, how to utilize it in sales presentations, and I gave a specific example of how it had already been used by The Elite Group in Southern California to get more sales presentations, and how it was opening doors that had been locked shut for years.

Out of nowhere, an inspector made a comment via the chat/question box about how he was familiar with The Elite Group, and how they did "really bad inspections." It was not a particularly unique comment; I get negative ones about inspectors all the time from their competition.

But this comment didn't come from Southern California. This statement was made by a home inspector on the East Coast.

Usually I just let the ignorant comments go, but in this particular case I went ahead and brought the comment up publicly.

What this inspector didn't know is that I have spent time with each of Elite Group's 35 home inspectors, spent more than a full week in their office, and worked directly with their inspection manager for years on quality control. They were also the first major home inspection company in the country to include *RecallChek* in their base inspection- only after a thorough discussion and market testing.

In other words, I know a lot about this company and I'm happy I do. They're the #1 inspection company in the country by volume from a single location. Nobody else serves more than 15,000 clients annually.

I went ahead and gave this inspector on the Webinar a chance to say his piece. I read his comment, didn't use his name, and then offered to unmute his microphone so he could enlighten us about how "bad" The Elite Group was personally. He didn't have a microphone on his computer (big surprise).

So I responded to his comment after reading it to the webinar attendees;

"You know guys, this is the kind of bullcrap that really hurts our industry. Here's an inspector, more than 2,000 miles away from another one, saying that an inspection company doesn't do a good, thorough inspection when he likely has no idea at all what's involved in an Elite Group inspection. He's almost certainly never seen one of their reports, never even possibly heard from one of their clients, it would be the same as me saying that he's an incompetent idiot and a walking liability, which he could very well be, I don't know, which is why I don't say it. I tend to think he's probably a good inspector, and I only hope he's as good as The Elite Group. Just to set the record straight, my company issues a 90-Day Warranty on every inspection The Elite Group does, and they have one of the lowest claim rates of *any* inspection company in North America. They're insured to a level most inspectors can't even afford and they haven't had a claim for as long as I've known them. Not only do I see their inspection reports but also I've personally been to an inspection with every single one of their more than 35 inspectors, and I would say they do as good a job as anybody out there, if not better. Oh, and by the way, I send out a *RecallChek* report to every single one of their clients and I have a folder in my *Outlook* full of responses from satisfied clients marked "The Elite Group". So unless you can show me 50+ e-mails from satisfied clients in your business from just last week alone, I'd suggest we take some important lessons from big, successful home inspection companies- because, let's be honest, the *only* reason this guy could have possibly had this opinion of The Elite Group is because he got it from another inspector who's in the same market as The Elite Group and he is getting his butt kicked."

Yes, our Webinars are very entertaining at times, but they are a "No B.S. Zone."

That night was the first time I truly understood how powerful the myth of the "bad" inspector was.

If you ask most inspectors what a "bad" inspector is, they'll likely start rattling off things like, "Inspectors who don't follow the Standards of Practice," or "Inspectors who do walk-through inspections."

You won't hear things like, "Inspectors who put out inspection reports that agents can't decipher."

You will hear, "Inspectors that miss things."

Well, show me an inspector who says he's never missed anything, and I'll show you the biggest liar in the room. We've all missed something.

This is why I have a slightly different definition for a "bad" inspector. I think an inspector who doesn't have a profitable business model is a bad inspector. I think an inspector who doesn't have the resources to resolve issues when they arise and provide a great life for their family is a "bad" inspector. I think an inspector who refuses to fix a $1,000 issue for a client referred by an agent who refers them $5,000 in business every year is making a bad business decision and is, in fact, a "bad" inspector. I think an inspector who thinks it's a good idea to offer the minimum service they have to and worries more about liability than growth is a "bad" inspector.

As an industry, we don't focus on the health of our businesses, but rather on how well one inspects.

##NEWSFLASH##

Nobody goes into home inspection for the money. They do it because they know about things mechanical and structural, they do it because they love inspecting, and almost nobody walks into the business with zero experience.

As I write this, I have more than 3,400 home inspectors on one of my programs. I see their reports, I hear from their clients, and I've worked with their insurance companies. I can't name you an inspector I know whom I wouldn't have inspect my own house.

If the way you promote yourself is that you're a "good, thorough inspector" and you are on a quest to save people from getting a bad inspection...I have an idea for you. This may be the best investment you could ever possibly make;

Get an inspection.

It may sound crazy, but this line of thinking that you are going to succeed because you are a good inspector and "everyone else sucks" is toxic. It will cost you literally hundreds of thousands of dollars over the remainder of your career.

So spend the $200-$500 now, and get a home inspection. Find a friend or family member, someone you can trust but has a different last name that has preferably purchased a home or several homes. Inspect their house, the same way you inspect every day. Produce a report. Then have your friend hire the other inspector to inspect the house. Have them tell the inspector that they are represented by a real estate agent, that they are currently renting the home and have made an offer to purchase it.

When you're done, put the inspections side by side, in front of your friend, but with all identifying marks taped over. Just sit there, listen as they go through the reports.

Of course there are exceptions, but I would say more than 99% of the time this experiment will result in both reports having every single major item ($500-$1000+ expense to repair) in common.

If every inspector did this, the myth of the "bad" inspector would be dispelled, and maybe we'd stop debating the proper way to install a toilet and start the discussion of how we take inspections to the next level. I'm not just referring to things like warranties, guarantees, RecallChek, or anything else I offer. I'm referring to things like new ways we could use IR and market it as a service, extended service and support for clients, and systems to keep in touch with past clients.

Maybe we could actually have the discussion as an industry of how we truly work better with real estate agents. How more of us could become a part of the real estate transaction without losing our integrity, our identity, or our desire to be thorough in everything we do.

Chapter 6
Pioneers Get Slaughtered

The first time I saw Dominic Maricic at a convention in Las Vegas, I had not heard of him before. I hadn't heard of Home Inspector Pro. All I knew was that here's a guy with Chuck Taylors, glasses, slim fit jeans, and a t-shirt selling something to inspectors. He was selling software, but talking about Google, and he was going on and on and on... and the inspectors weren't leaving!

I had to interrupt him to introduce myself.

That's Dominic's style. You go up to his booth, ask him anything about Website design, Google rankings, or any other related topic and he will talk about it until you decide to walk away. Maybe you're a client of his, maybe you're not, it doesn't matter. He's going to educate you.

He's the opposite of what you would think inspectors would gravitate towards, but they come in droves.

Why?

His stuff works. It just works.

There are a multitude of ways to get your Website up and going, and there are even some other great providers in the industry- but I see Dominic as *the* catalyst behind the inspection industry's Web domination.

Typical home inspections run around $300. The typical homebuyer purchases one house every seven years. More than 80% of homebuyers will go with the first inspector recommended by their real estate agent. That leaves less than 20% of around five million homebuyers each year in the U.S. and Canada who will be shopping for a home inspector, and while many of them will do an Internet search, it's still an incredibly small market.

In fact, I would challenge you to find any industry with as many participants in the Internet marketing game. Search just about any city on Google, combine that with "home inspection", "home inspector", or "inspection," and you're going to find both paid ads at the top of the page as well as natural results that lead directly to an inspector's Website. Pages and pages of them. Do the same search for appliance repair, all you get is responses from Yelp and Service Magic and the like. There are probably 20 times as many appliance repairs as home inspections each year, and nearly all of those homeowners are shopping for a service provider. That makes the Internet market in appliance repair more than 80 times as big as home inspection yet home inspectors are light years ahead.

Vendors like Dominic make it easy, and my advice is simple. Spend some money; get your Website up and ranked on Google. Also, *don't rely on your Website and client referrals to be your sole sources of business.*

The problem with Web sites that drive some inspection business is that they drive "some" business. They offer a glimmer of hope to inspectors that don't want to put the hard work into establishing a real estate-transaction-friendly product, and don't want to actually get out and do the hard work of marketing their service. Let the Website do all the work.

This is where the Web pioneers in our industry are getting hurt *big time*. Every inspector is capable of doing 500, 600, even 1,000 inspections per year and make really good money doing it. Once you get to a certain point, you can create systems that work and start hiring inspectors. It's called running a business. But if you get your share of the small amount of inspections out there being booked as a result of Web searches, you get a distorted view of what success looks like.

Fact: There is not an inspection company in the country doing $1 million+ in revenue with any significant portion of it coming from their Website.

It doesn't mean that these companies don't have Websites. Doesn't mean they don't pay for ads or spend money and resources on getting ranked on Google.

It just means that they don't let the rare homebuyer who doesn't trust their agent's recommendations define their business.

There are literally hundreds of home inspectors who have absolutely mastered the art of luring in these paranoid exceptions. I'm truly impressed, but at the same time I feel sorry for some of them who don't realize that by making these statements on their Website and even at the inspection about how clients should trust them over anyone recommended by their agent is really just alienating them from real estate offices and making them look really bad. They're the same kind of inspectors who inadvertently say to buyers every once in awhile "I wouldn't buy this house!" (Even if they didn't use those words precisely.)

It's the marketing equivalent of a bear trap in home inspection, and chatter on the inspection forums and at local inspector events multiplies its effects.

"I got an inspection yesterday from my Website...and I didn't have to worry about impressing the damn real estate agent!"

Misguided statements like this make the inspector the envy of his peers, or at least some of them. The statement should really be better qualified or expanded. It would make things more honest, because nobody will speak up and ask the necessary questions, the business questions that should be asked. For instance, how many of these appointments are you booking per day? How many agent referrals do you get per day? (The answers to these questions are incredibly unimpressive)

The really good inspection business owners out there don't rely on Web promotion. They know that 80%+ of their business should come from agent referrals. The other 20% that comes from their Website is just gravy.

Chapter 7
A True Marketing Message

From Baltimore to L.A., Chicago to Dallas, everywhere I go there are car washes within a few miles. Some of them are automatic machines, others are spray hoses you need a pocketful of quarters to operate. Then there are some that have people who dry your car off by hand, or even use mops and pre-rinse your car before you go into the machine. Like anything else, prices vary, but basic washes cost from $3 to $10 and usually end up somewhere in the middle, with one glaring exception.

Mike's Express Carwash is a company in Indiana that sells automated car washes for $18, the going rate for the "Works" wash with "Tire Shine."

You read right. There's no hand drying, nothing done to the interior at all. They just roll your car through what might feel like any other automatic carwash. You stay in your car while it happens.

It's a good carwash, but is it the best? I don't know. Is it worth the money? No clue. Are they the busiest, fastest-growing carwash in the country? You bet.

Between radio, TV, billboards, and locations in every part of town, they're ubiquitous. I've seen $2 coupons print out on the back of a grocery receipt towards a Mike's Express Carwash at my local Kroger.

I'm almost certain that the owners of this company make millions of dollars and it's a good thing they took the advice of business consultants and learned the lessons other big businesses had instead of asking another carwash owner.

If they had listened to another carwash owner, they might have received some advice that is good, but not great. They might have heard about which carwash machines deliver the best carwash, or which ones do it the quickest, or maybe which ones have the lowest maintenance cost and are the easiest for staff to operate.

They might have been lucky enough to get some good advice about location and signage two of the biggest drivers of business for most carwashes.

You don't perform thousands or even tens of thousands of carwashes per day at dozens of locations, each costing I would estimate around $2 million to build, by following advice from single-location owner-operators who serve only hundreds of customers monthly. If you listen to them, you'd probably get some really bad advice like, "If you just do the best wash you can, people will come back and tell their friends and you'll have a great carwash business."

By Mike's Express standards, following this line of thinking would result in a colossal failure.

That doesn't mean they don't offer a great carwash. They certainly don't strive to offer a mediocre one. Their customer service is amazing, but they have a lot of customers to serve and that's the key.

For most carwash owners, spending money on marketing is tough to do. They don't get a huge return, so they trickle their marketing efforts out slowly attempting to gain a customer whom they can turn into a repeat client and see a return...then they trickle out some more. Most of their marketing says two things:

1. Their location.

2. That they offer a great carwash.

Hopefully, in their marketing they focused on the hyper-local area so that location of the recipients of the message mattered a *lot*. The second part of the message is meaningless. It would be the same as a home inspector saying, "I do a good inspection." Of course they're going to say they have a good carwash.

Mike's does things differently. It's almost like there are people running the company who not only know how to wash a car, but also know how to run a business!

The message is simple: Mike's is the best carwash *because:*

- 1,000,0000 BTU water heaters. It doesn't matter whether you're the first car or the last car of the day or anywhere in between, you're going to get hot water.

- More blowers than any other carwash- and at higher power too! Your car will be dry!

- Buy "The Book"- Get six washes for the price of five and you can use them at any of their locations.

Then you show up and find a consistently sized, brick building, complete with all the vacuums and ancillary services you're looking for. Oh, and every associate is wearing a uniform with a tie. A tie at a carwash!

The guy down the street may offer a better carwash, but I will never know.

If you think home inspection is different than literally every other business in the world, then you need to just accept your place as a low-volume provider of service at market rates.

Home inspection is no different than other businesses- it's just incredibly fragmented and full of technicians, many of whom would be happy to work for someone else if they could actually be guaranteed a salary and benefits.

By following the standard SOP and not offering anything substantially different from your competition, you become inexpensive Vodka- served from the well of the bar to people that don't realize or don't have the means to understand that life is too short for bottom shelf liquor.

Chapter 8
Liability and Lies

Wool carpet in a solid color doesn't seem on its face to be a big deal. Frankly, I'm not a big fan. Give me hardwoods, slate, travertine, or even a really good carpet and I'm happy, but in the McMansions of Carmel, Indiana there are quite a few $2 million + houses that have wool carpeting. Expensive wool carpeting.

On one of those minor detours in my life between the last time I was fired by my parents and before I took over the home warranty company, I started a little property services business. Eventually I figured out that the most money to be made was in big contracts with management companies, which ultimately led to my being able to sell that company less than a year after starting it for pretty decent money at the time. But before I figured that out I went for the home runs in the form of McMansions.

I left fliers, made phone calls, offered everything from cleaning gutters to changing light bulbs and doing general maintenance to housekeeping services. Since most people don't trust their home maintenance needs to an eighteen-year-old who looks not a day over fifteen, I picked up a bunch of housekeeping clients.

What a pain in the butt.

I was still in high school, so I would assemble my staff in the mornings, I had around ten people within two months of starting the service, and I would assign them their jobs, and then I would check on them in-between classes.

There was one house I'll never forget. Probably a $1.7 million house at the time in 1999. It was around 12,000 square feet, half a dozen kids lived there, and the client was extremely particular about how things were cleaned. She would watch the team of three I'd send over there ever Wednesday, two of whom couldn't speak English well.

It made them nervous.

Especially nervous was the newcomer to the group, his name escapes me. He was cleaning an upstairs bathroom, and it was right off this sizeable "bridge" between the master bedroom and the other bedrooms spanning the dramatic two plus story entryway.

He was using a bleach-based cleaner in the bathroom and he was being watched. He was looking away as he put the bottle down into his bucket, and he missed. The bottle hit the carpeting, the brownish-orange designer *wool* carpeting. At first it appeared just wet apparently. Over a period of about an hour it got lighter, and lighter, and then white as the perfect ring the size of the bottom of the bottle now showed brightly on what I thought was an otherwise ugly carpet.

I carried two cell phones in high school. One was forwarded from my office line so I never missed a call, the other for employees (and friends/family I suppose) to call me on. They both vibrated in my pocket, I excused myself from class to go to the bathroom (a.k.a. my "office"), and I took the call from the office line first.

It was the high-maintenance, pain in the butt homeowner.

She was bouncing off the walls, furious. I calmed her down, let her know it's just carpet, no big deal, we'll take care of it.

"But it's specialty carpet!"

I didn't argue with her, I just told her to get an estimate to fix it and get me a copy so I can look at it. I spoke to my employees, found out what happened, and the bottom line was this: I was responsible.

I was new to the business. I didn't want a big claim on my general liability insurance, but this shouldn't be a big deal. A couple hundred bucks, maybe?

Try $4,600.

$4,600 for some stupid wool carpet in what can't be a 200 square foot area, and of course no way they could patch it in.

You can do a lot with $4,600. You can replace both a furnace and an air conditioner. You can put a new roof on most houses. You can fix a major structural issue. You can mitigate the home for radon, treat it for termites, and have money to spare for a vacation.

$4,600 was a lot of money to an eighteen-year-old running his first business. I had payroll to meet, a mortgage to pay, and an addiction to fast cars to pursue. As painful as it was, I committed to take care of the issue.

Ultimately I found a company that specializes in coloring high-end carpeting, and the issue was resolved for less than $1,000. Had I not answered the client's phone calls, had I not committed to *solving the problem*, the client may not have accepted the repair.

I owe that to my parents and how they ran the business I grew up in. White Ford Rangers with blue logos, uniformed inspectors, letterhead and business cards, and computer-generated reports before anybody else in the business even had a computer. They answered the call before the third ring every time, and no they were not afraid to solve a problem even if it meant writing a check.

I'm not even positive when they started in the business that Errors and Omissions insurance for inspectors was available. I know it was uncommon. Very early on they did thousands of inspections each year when most of their competition did less than a hundred, and every once in a while there was a complaint. Less often, the complaint turned into a threat of legal action. Seldom, those threats turned into reality and what you've heard from other inspectors about that limitation of liability in the inspection agreement not necessarily holding up in court is absolutely true. It does sometimes, but not all the time.

The rule for us was simple: you don't go to court if you're in the wrong. Period.

So while other kids my age were enjoying being "kids", I was dressing professionally, printing up business cards, printing out professional invoices, and answering the phone every time it rang.

If this homeowner had been dealing with anyone else twice my age, they would have likely not accepted the repair. Liability has little to do with standards of practice or with contracts. These things are important, but the real test in the client's mind is how comfortable they feel throughout the process (your level of professionalism) and your response to their complaints.

Let's look at the various ways you can look professional, versus the less professional opposite:

Professional- The client calls to book an inspection, gets a professional phone answering staff member who takes their information, gets them scheduled, and then sends them a confirmation e-mail along with the inspection agreement and a detailed written proposal as to what the inspection includes. The phone is answered, "Thank you for calling Professional Home Inspections, this is Nicole, how may I help you?"

Unprofessional- Client calls and gets the inspector himself who answers the phone, or maybe a voice-mail that even says which cell phone service he uses and gets a call back. The inspector proceeds to take the order with background noise clearly indicating he is not in an office. There is no e-mail follow-up, and the person who answered the phone is the same person who shows up to do the inspection. The phone is answered, "Jim's Home Inspection Service".

The first company exudes confidence and professionalism. The client now has the name of not only the inspector, but also someone who works in the office at this professional organization they'd never heard of before they were referred by their real estate agent or found them on the Web. They feel good and know that if they have a question or an issue that they can call the business phone number any time, talk to a person, and get their issues resolved.

The second company, in this case "Jim" (he's the entire "company" in the client's mind, and it's never a good idea to have a word like "company" in quotation marks), has destroyed any possibility that he will ever be a true professional in the client's mind. The best he can hope for is a personal relationship and level of trust that he might be able to create once on-site, but that's about it.

This is where liability starts. After the inspection, after the closing, after the move-in, and after something doesn't work correctly, people have a tendency to want to get things fixed. If they have an air conditioning issue and they call a company with a big advertisement in the yellow pages, they're going to get a professional response. When that contractor then shows up in a big painted truck in a uniform with a professional bid for replacing the air conditioner for some ridiculously large sum of money, you're already behind the eight ball. When that company says (erroneously) that "Your inspector should have told you this thing needed to be replaced"…The client believes him!

If you were just as professional, showed up in a truck with your logo on it, had an office staff or a call center that made you look professional before you even showed up, you would be on a level playing field.

It doesn't matter what type of contractor we're talking about. It could be a plumber, a termite treatment company, a structural contractor, or a mold remediation firm- it doesn't matter. When people experience a problem, they don't automatically call an attorney and sue their home inspector. They have to have a reason to, and they have to go through a few stages to get there:

1. First Impression- was the inspector just an *inspector* with a truck, or was this a professional home inspection company with the resources to handle my issues?

2. Problem Found, Now What? – What do I do when there's a problem? Can I call the inspection company and get an immediate answer to my concern or will I just get the inspector's cell phone voice-mail? Will he even return my call in time for this problem to be resolved before it causes more problems in my life?

3. Where's the process? – When I called the contractor, they told me I should definitely go after the inspector for this. That if *they* had missed [fill in defect here] they would take care of it. So is there a process for handling this, or do I just get it

taken care of and deal with it later as the contractor suggests?

4. Demand- A request has been made to solve the client's problem. Whether it is a real problem or not has already been determined in their mind through stages 1, 2, & 3.

5. Resolution- The issue has either been resolved in the client's mind or it hasn't. If it hasn't, they continue to be active in seeking resolution.

There are a few frivolous exceptions to any of this, but short of the rare individual who is actually out to get you, acknowledgement of these stages and building systems to avert complaints every step of the way is a sure-fire way to reduce liability.

None of this relieves the need to have a good, solid contract or to be well versed in the minimum Standards of Practice, but the number one way to reduce liability is to be "more than just an inspector," be a *company*.

Let me give you an example outside of the inspection business. Let's say you bought a car from a small car lot, the kind that doesn't have a brand affiliation like Penske or Tom Wood or Germain or whoever is the big car dealer in your area with brand affiliations and multiple dealerships. You purchased from the kind of car lot that doesn't have an indoor showroom and does not sell new cars.

They had the car you wanted; it's a used Ford Mustang for this example. You test drive the car, you buy it cash, and you take it home.

The next day the engine seizes.

What do you do?

I think most people might call the dealer, tell them about the issue, and see what they're willing to do about it.

What if they don't answer the phone?

What if they tell you that you bought the car "As-Is," no warranty?

What do you do next?

A few Google searches, maybe a call to an attorney or two, and about 24 hours of completely stressing out later, you'll come across your state's "Lemon Law," that usually says something to the effect that if you buy a total piece of garbage and it falls apart within seven days, the dealer either has to fix it or buy it back.

Now that you know the law exists, you confront the dealer about it, and they say, "Oh, we'll fix it."

You drop off the car and wait. Days pass. A week passes. No word.

It's clear that the dealer doesn't have the backing to deal with the issue, so they're likely shopping some hole in the wall auto shops trying to find someone to fix this issue on the cheap, which doesn't mean they're fixing it "well."

This is of course nothing more than a theory on your part, but it's building up in the form of stomach acid until you finally call them and ask for your money back.

"We're fixing it, be patient."

Eventually you sue them for the sticker price of the car, and they don't show up in court. Then you pay your attorney (again) for a "proceedings supplemental" to actually collect on your default judgment, which only goes so far because you can't squeeze juice out of a turnip.

What if this whole issue was nothing but a simple fix, and there was legitimately a backup of service at the auto repair shop they took it to? What if they chose a mechanic who was known to be the best in the business at working on that year, make and model of car, and they genuinely wanted to get it fixed right for you?

None of that mattered.

They lost your confidence the minute the salesperson was also the finance guy and was also the guy to clean out the car and also the guy to handle your call when you had a complaint and you assume he was also the guy who bought the car at an auction in the first place.

Zero structure + Zero staff= Zero consumer confidence.

This is how many clients are made to feel almost immediately when they order a home inspection at most home inspection companies. Think about it.

Now let's take the same example from above, except you bought a used car at the largest dealership in town. Same thing happened. You brought it home and the engine seized. You call the dealership, explain the situation, they put you in contact with a service manager.

He has you bring the car in, they want to check it out and see what they can do.

They find the minor issue that appears to you like it is seizing, fix it, you pick up the car, and everything is fine.

Does it cost them some money to resolve these sorts of issues? Yes. Do they invest a lot of money in staff and resources to be able to handle complaints in this manner? You betcha. Do they have a better reputation and higher confidence from consumers in their products and have more repeat business? Oh yes. Do they charge more for their used cars than the tiny car lots out there and make bigger profits? Absolutely!

As a home inspection company owner, you have to make the decision as to whether you want to look like a greasy, low end used car dealer or a pristine, world-class, high end dealership.

How do you do that?

Simple. If you have more than three inspectors, hire someone to work as your office manager and answer the phones. If you have less than three inspectors, hire a call center. There are two of them listed in the resources section in the back of this book, and they're the only two in North America that specifically handle home inspection call center services (if you're a franchisee, there may be additional options for you).

The other thing you need to do is have scripts. How you answer the phone every time it rings. "Jim's Home Inspection" is not a proper call answering script, and if you think I'm being harsh just go seek advice from counsel on your future bankruptcy now.

Try something more like, "Thank you for calling Security Home Inspection, this is Nathan, how may I help you?" I've only repeated those words tens of thousands of times. I could walk into that office right now and I would almost automatically reach for the phone when it rang and if I didn't stop myself I'd end up saying that to the person on the other line.

The final thing to do is to leave your ego at the door. If you're still in the field inspecting, and that's a good use of your time, when you're on site you are *not* the owner, the president of the company, or any other such nonsense. You are the inspector.

Print up business cards that say it. Wear a uniform. Install logos on your truck. Be a humble servant to your clients on inspections the way you want every inspector that ever works for you or carries on the business after you to do.

Then establish processes for dealing with complaints, a hierarchy to make sure clients have confidence in the process, and a policy that issues are tended to quickly, resolved efficiently, and dealt with before they cause the biggest liability of all, the one that happens a thousand times as often as an inspector going to court, losing future clients and referrals.

Chapter 9
The USP

Domino's Pizza, in 2011-2012, came out with an ad campaign they ran nationally that I like to call "Our Pizza Sucks!...But We're Fixing It." It was an interesting concept, and the results seem to indicate it worked. They would put people in a room, hand them a slice of Domino's pizza, and then show their negative reactions. Next they showed their pizza chefs fixing the problem, delivering the new and improved pizza to a participant in the study's front door, and the positive response to the new flavors.

The ads were brilliantly done, zooming in and focusing on the herbs and spices they put on the crust and boasting about improvements they had made to toppings. The first pizza I bought after I saw these ads was from Domino's.

Maybe you like the pizza, maybe you don't, but Domino's has some of the best marketing people in the world working at their corporate headquarters. In one of the most competitive foodservice industry sectors, Domino's skyrocketed past almost everybody to become the #2 pizza delivery company in the world.

They were able to do this for two main reasons; 1. They had a solid business plan. 2. They were the only pizza delivery company to differentiate themselves.

Domino's figured it out in 1973. They made themselves stand out in the marketplace by offering a guarantee that, "if you don't get your pizza in 30 minutes or less, it's free!"

This was revolutionary, and it scared the heck out of their competitors. In boardrooms and offices of the other pizza brands you could hear the shouts of executives losing market share, making excuses for not being able to offer the same guarantee.

"But what if we have to give a pizza away for free?"

"What if we get too many orders?"

Domino's did give away some free pizzas, but they sold more pizzas than everybody else, so who cares if they had to give away a free one here or there? It didn't add up to much.

They didn't have any problems keeping up with the demand or offering the guarantee in multiple countries. However, eventually there were some accidents involving Domino's delivery drivers and public perception of the guarantee had turned from gleeful to skeptical that drivers might be pushed to drive less than safely. The number of accidents they had weren't any worse than other pizza brands, it was nothing more than a perception issue and they were becoming a target for lawsuits as a result. *That wasn't until 1993 that they temporarily halted the guarantee-* and then in 2007 they brought the guarantee back in a slightly different form, because as it turns out differentiating yourself from the competition is a pretty darn profitable thing to do.

What do others in the pizza business do? They say they have good pizza, and then they try to be price competitive. That's it.

At least when it comes to food there are discernable differences in flavor. Some people prefer Pizza Hut or Papa John's for the taste, but if you asked the average consumer why they chose any particular pizza over another, you'd probably find that they weren't loyal to any particular brand. But in the late 80's and early 90's, during the period of Domino's largest growth, the answer was really simple: "Domino's delivers fast."

The *"delivered in 30 minutes or it's free"* campaign was what is known as a Unique Selling Proposition or a "USP." The term was invented by Rosser Reeves of Ted Bates & Company in the 1940's, and it was first introduced as a theory of why advertising campaigns of the time were successful in getting consumers to switch from one brand to another.

In order for a theory to be a *Unique Selling Proposition* it must be one that others in the same business don't or can't offer. It must have the power to move the masses to your product or service, and it must say to the potential buyer of your products or services that "if you buy this product or service, you'll get this benefit".

It's sometimes referred to by the unenlightened as a "gimmick."

If you're in a service business like home inspection, you need to have offerings that make you *unique*. If you don't, every dollar you spend on Web development, Google ads, or printing of fliers and business cards is wasted. You're just another home inspector who wants their business.

In the early days of Security Home Inspections, it wasn't hard to be unique. Most inspection companies didn't have an office that answered the phone and delivered reports and visited every real estate office in town regularly. Showing up and answering the phone and being a "real" business were enough to leave the competition in the dust.

As time passed, more inspectors were catching on to the importance of looking professional, so Security Home Inspections did some things that few inspectors had the resources to do. My dad spent the money and time he needed to in order to get a plumbing license, and my mother got her pest control operator's license. She was one of the only women in the classes, and the only person in the room who had no intention of offering treatment for termites and other wood destroying organisms at all- and likewise my dad was the only one in the room that didn't even own a plumber's torch.

It may have been expensive and painful at the time, but Security Home Inspections became the company that you could make *one call* to and get all of your home inspection needs done. They could now offer inspections, wood destroying pest reports, well and septic inspections, and water testing.

Real estate agents responded well to this concept. They didn't have to hand a client five or six different companies to call and get these different inspections arranged and *hope* their clients got all of these tests completed before the inspection response period expired. Security Home Inspections could also offer these tests for less than if you hired three or four different parties because they were already there, so the home buyers saw an immediate benefit in a reduction of costs in purchasing a home. Profits went up too.

Time passed and once again innovation was needed in order to stay ahead of the pack, and in 2001 Security Home Inspections became our first 90-Day Warranty client.

The pitch was simple, and once again their profit margins and market share went up. "With every full inspection we perform, you get a 90-Day Warranty so that even if something like your dishwasher is working perfectly fine at the time of your inspection, if you move in and it has a problem, you can call the warranty company and get it fixed."

This was their best USP to date, because it scared the heck out of their competition and made them look terrible at the same time. Prospective clients would call around to the three companies their agents referred them to, and after they called Security Home Inspections they would ask the next company not about their *price*, but rather if they offered a warranty with their home inspections.

Some inspectors were smart and just said "No." They still didn't book the inspection, but at least they didn't do what some others did and start lecturing the client about what an inspection is and that warranties aren't a part of their standards, etc.

After getting that lecture, more than one inspection company was actually removed from agents' referral lists because the clients didn't like being talked down to.

After several years, others in the marketplace started offering 90-Day Warranties, but still less than 10% of inspectors. The 90-Day Warranty remains today a USP that makes you different than most all of your competitors, and when implemented properly it renders any sales pitch a competitor might have useless. I'm fairly decent with words, and I can't figure out how to convince someone that *not* having a warranty is better than having one.

The 90-Day Warranty is not the only way to make your company unique, there are endless possibilities. There are offerings from vendors like myself like RecallChek, discounts on alarm monitoring systems, and Termite Protection Plans, and then there are things you can put in place yourself. Some inspectors give each client a book on how to operate their home- some of these publications are original, some are purchased from third parties and there are several other sources listed in the resources section of this book. Some inspection companies offer free re-inspections (also referred to as "repair inspections"). Some offer them for a small fee and that's perfectly fine as well.

At Security Home Inspections, we always charged for our re-inspections but many of our competitors didn't offer them at all. It was great to hear the excuses... "I don't do re-inspections, I do inspections. If you want me to re-inspect a home, I'll do it for the full inspection fee because I don't know what else might have changed in the home."

When I was answering the phone for Security Home Inspections, on more than one occasion I had a buyer ask me if I would match the price of a particular competitor who I knew didn't offer re-inspections. *Every single time* I not only booked the order but did so at our full fee. All I had to do was tell the client the following:

"Ah, yes, [inspection company name], I'm somewhat familiar with them. They're a small operation I think on the west side, pretty new I believe. We don't match prices with anyone. Most companies know we're the market leader and tend to come in right below our pricing for that reason. One thing you might want to consider is that after we do the inspection and you have the seller make corrections, we offer to re-inspect those services and make sure they were repaired properly before you close on the house, and the fee for that is only $95- it's something I would recommend you consider doing. Any inspector confident in his abilities in inspecting your home should also be familiar with repair standards and all of our inspectors are familiar with those standards. If [inspection company name] doesn't offer re-inspections you should call them to find out why. I personally don't see why someone familiar with home systems wouldn't be capable of offering this service for you."

I let that company do the rest of the selling for me.

Other Unique Selling Propositions used to include things like computer-generated reports and color digital photographs, but those are pretty standard now. By "standard" I mean to say "required."

I know of an inspector in Texas that after you get an inspection and move in, gets your lawn mowed for free.

Sound crazy? I won't name names but they're doing pretty darn well.

Some inspectors offer free pool and irrigation system inspections, which has the dual benefit of giving them the ability to increase their base inspection fees and the ability to target higher end homes (and agents). *Some inspectors don't like doing things for free, but if your base rate increases and your volume does as well- it's not really "free."*

Some inspectors (around 10% of them) offer RecallChek and check for recalls on every home they inspect, plus check for recalls every month for their clients for as long as they own their home. Nearly all of these inspectors charge more than their competition every day, and about a quarter of those inspectors pay nothing for this service.

Those same inspectors offer free e-mail newsletters from the agents to their clients.

Maybe none of these differentiators are for you or for your business and that's fine. Maybe you're going to be the inspector who revolutionizes the business for the next generation of inspectors.

Just don't go *backwards*.

Backwards takes us to one place and that's irrelevance sprinkled with poverty. When my parents did their first inspections, in the infancy of the industry, the inspection fees were in the $90 range, inspections took 45 minutes, and they were garbage. By today's standards, the inspections of thirty years ago would be seen as far from adequate. Today, average fees at the same company top $500, and nationally run around $300. *Imagine 30 years from today when most inspectors are checking for recalls, offering guarantees, and utilizing advanced tools in their inspection process like infrared cameras...we'll be talking about how "inadequate" inspections in 2012 were!*

When inspection companies come up with a new offering, they should be applauded. We should all hope that it takes hold, and adds to all of our bottom lines. Even the mediocre inspector with less business savvy than the five year old running your neighborhood lemonade stand owes the innovators of the early years for being competitive and taking the electrical panel cover off, buying a ladder and using it to get on the roof, and creating software in Access or FileMaker or buying it from Carl Fowler at 3-D. If they had not done these things, if they had been influenced at all at the time by those who called their trucks with ladders and computerized reports "gimmicks," then we would still be doing incomplete, inadequate, and cheap 45-minute home inspections.

Chapter 10
The Mike Crow Effect

Carleton H. Sheets reigned supreme in late night infomercials for two decades. It's estimated that the total cost for airtime ran the company that promoted him around $280 million. That's a lot of airtime, and if you don't know who Carleton Sheets is and you work in this business, you need to learn a little bit about this real estate industry we work in.

His system was called *No Money Down*, and it was a guide to investing in real estate. There were books, audio books, CD's, and, of course, you could pay to attend one of Carleton's presentations as well.

Today, the world of real estate investing info-marketers is in shambles.

We all saw the infomercials, and many of us laughed at them. It must be "too good to be true." It's not believable.

We see on the screen examples of not-so-well-spoken individuals who are "students" of Carleton sitting next to their pool in front of their yacht and talking about how easy it is to make millions in real estate if we just follow Carleton's system.

Critics of Sheets and the half a billion dollars in sales he generated say that the method of selling the system was targeted at the naïve. This may be so, but that doesn't mean his system didn't have validity. In fact, there was a lot of sound advice he gave his "students."

How do I know?

Because I listened to every single audiotape he recorded his books and systems onto.

It wasn't by choice; this was happening between the ages of nine and twelve that I had to put up with it because back in those days there wasn't a separate entertainment system in the back of every mom-mobile like there is now. Every tape of Carleton's monotone voice, the Mr. Rogers of real estate, was played in my mother's van for three years straight.

My parents weren't naïve. They were very smart and they knew that Carleton Sheets was being listened to by 100's of thousands of real estate investors (a.k.a. "potential clients"), and they wanted to know more about their clients than anyone else. That way they could speak intelligently on investment issues when they were brought up by agents and clients alike. Maybe Sheets wasn't the only source, but he was a good starting point.

They picked up some great advice on real estate investing. They went on to pick up a few more resources, spoke to their bankers and attorneys, and started buying properties.

There were undoubtedly a large majority of Carleton Sheets students who had no idea what they were doing, or didn't follow the system, or both, that got into trouble making bad investments or didn't even buy a single house.

On the other end of the spectrum, there were thousands of people like my parents who took his system, perfected it for their own uses, and went to town building wealth in real estate. If my parents ever decide to retire, they can do so to their choice of multiple properties they hold in sunny, sandy, beach and island locations. What suckers they are for spending almost $500 on the full "No Money Down" system!

By the time I graduated high school, I had already purchased two properties. One was the house in which I lived and had significant equity in, the other was a condo I had rented out and was cash-flowing quite nicely. Both had been purchased without any involvement from my parents, I'm not sure they would have been very supportive of my plans if I had ever told them, but I had the knowledge, much of which had come from those Carleton Sheets tapes.

That's why it makes no sense that to this day I am the most skeptical person I know. I still watch infomercials and laugh. I still see "coaches" and "consultants" as a waste of time and money.

It's why I understand completely why some of the home inspectors who see Mike Crow do one of his presentations will later say, "He's full of it. Why would I pay him for his advice?" I also understand why some inspectors won't listen to him at all.

It took me a good long conversation with myself before I finally decided to put this chapter in the book. There's a certain *risk* to telling anyone what he or she ought to hear. It's kind of like seeing someone (much bigger and angrier than you) drinking in a bar and suggesting that they stop before drink number eleven and ask them for the keys to the car you saw them drive up in. It's the right thing to do. I've done it on multiple occasions, but sometimes they take a swing at you or get even angrier.

There's nothing you can do for them.

You, on the other hand, have made it pretty far through a pretty intense book that not a lot of stubborn, petty, unsuccessful inspectors are going to like so I have confidence that you can handle this statement:

Try Mike Crow's system, spend a few hundred bucks, and if it's not for you stop.

It's not for everybody. There were hundreds of thousands of people who completely failed on Carleton Sheets' systems, but thousands of others who thrived.

I think the numbers are at least a little better when it comes to Mike Crow's members of his "Millionaire Inspector Community." I *know* they are- because we track those numbers. *I think the name of his group is as cheesy as you might-* and so do many of his members by the way. It's all very intentionally outrageous.

Here's another statement I think you can probably handle:

Sixteen of the top 25 Inspector Services Group clients are members of Mike Crow's organization, and those companies on average do more than *15 times* as many inspections as the average inspector in the U.S. and Canada.

Several of the other companies in that top 25 list have been a member of Mike's organization at one time or another. Some of them like his stuff and just didn't need him anymore...they had "graduated" in their minds. Others didn't like the advice, or left for other reasons. Push comes to shove, all of them would likely say the return on investment was good.

It's hard to believe that the statistical domination these companies all have in common over their competition is a coincidence.

You may think it's all bull, and that's okay. Just because you don't subscribe to Mike Crow's, or anyone else's stuff for that matter doesn't make you unsuccessful or unintelligent. You might even feel "stupid" for needing help growing your business. You would probably feel like a fool for ordering Carleton Sheets' system in the late 80's or early 90's, but it *might* have been the best thing that ever happened to you. It might have inspired you to do something, even if you didn't take the specific advice and implement it.

That's the way it works with Mike's stuff as well, but if his style isn't your cup of tea, find something that is. Get involved in a mastermind group, bring in a consultant, or even get someone from outside the profession to work with you on a growth strategy.

I once spent $4,000 to go to one seminar. I also spent over $25,000 for three days of consulting.

Laugh if you want to.

I would estimate my returns from those two spenditures, totaling less than $30,000, to be a number I'm not even comfortable publishing. I've also sought the advice of Mike Crow on many occasions, and not once was I disappointed with the results.

No, I won't tell you what Mike Crow's advice is. Not because I'm bound by any sort of confidentiality, it's more a matter of the information needing to be presented in a certain way in order for it to be effective. In other words, I could tell you a few things and you could use the advice in a way that doesn't help you and may even hurt you.

I will tell you this: 80% of what Mike says is common sense stuff that everyone should be doing but we often forget and need that motivation to keep up on the basics. The other 20% is cutting edge stuff to keep you ahead of the competition. Some of it works great, some of it is so-so. You won't know until you implement it and every market is a little different.

A few hundred dollars buys you the full experience for a couple of months, take from it what you want to. He'll send you a package and invite you to some conference calls. I personally know over a hundred inspectors who have seen double and even triple digit growth in their volume *and* revenue with Mike. Probably half of them needed the information and the other half already knew most of it but couldn't put together an organized plan of attack without some guidance.

I've also seen the same from clients who implement our products and services, I've seen it from franchisees of HouseMaster, Pillar to Post, HomeTeam, WIN, and others as well.

It's really about having a mindset that allows you to take advantage of the systems and experiences of others. Give Mike Doerr in my office twenty minutes of your time and see what he can do for your Website. If you're a franchisee, grab every resource you can from corporate.

If you would rather take on the world yourself and be a one-man army, good for you. I used to be that guy, and I was proud of what I did every day regardless of the results. Just be prepared to make every mistake everyone else has made getting to where they are.

You may never get where you want to be, but at least you did it your way!

Chapter 11
Agent Haters

If it weren't for my grandfather's love of the great American steak, I would not be here today.

It may seem like a strange statement, but *Don Thornberry's Steak Place* was a legendary restaurant in Carmel, Indiana. To this day I still run into people who ate there almost weekly and got personal visits at their table from Don.

After running the most profitable *Bonanza* restaurant in the country, my grandfather opened an independent steak house right on the main road running through Carmel. It was a noticeable feature in the landscape, and as a good supporter of the community, he sponsored things like the Carmel High School yearbook, even though his oldest son and very decent grill worker, Phil (my father), went to a private high school in Indianapolis.

I'm not sure if it was the location of the restaurant or one of the advertisements that drove a girl named Patty to go and apply, but she did, and that steak house is where she met Phil, and even though they were only in high school at the time, they eventually married and had me at a relatively young age.

I eat steak almost every day religiously.

Probably not the best choice for my body or longevity, but everything good that ever happened to me started with a steak as far as I'm concerned.

Including an incredible real estate career for Don.

My grandfather later became a real estate agent and worked with a couple of big firms, ultimately at two of the largest Re/Max franchises in the state.

The relationships he had made as a proprietor in the restaurant business and his incredible negotiation skills led him to eventually get a couple of enormous builder contracts. To this day he's got one of the highest all-time sales records in the entire industry. Out of the 1.5 million active real estate agents in the country today, you might find a handful who sell the volume of real estate he did each year, and he kept it up for decades.

I was lucky enough to be the eldest of the grandchildren by a long shot, and as such I probably had more time with Grandpa Don before he died than my brothers or cousins did, which I will be eternally grateful for.

He was a pilot, a boater, an entrepreneur many times over, and probably had the highest level of integrity of anyone I've ever met.

"Don't do anything you wouldn't want on the front page of the newspaper the next day," he would tell me.

When you sell as much real estate as he did, you have the pleasure of interacting with pretty much anybody selling homes in the area. Spending days with him over the summers, I would be in his home office as he was dealing with the latest issue standing between his seller or buyer and the closing of a deal. Most of the time, all parties were civil and easy to deal with. Occasionally, there were fireworks as one of the parties redefined "crazy."

Being there from the start of a transaction to the very end, witnessing tens of millions of dollars in transactions in a single summer season (with occasional breaks for a matinee and McDonald's), you begin to understand what agents truly deal with.

The ignorant views of some inspectors who seem to think that many agents in the profession would just as soon sweep a structural issue under the rug and let their clients deal with the consequences later just aren't true.

Since those summers, between our one-year warranties, 90-Day Warranties, RecallChek reports, Radon Protection Plans, Termite Protection Plans, and other services we offer, I've been on some level involved in around $300 Billion in real estate transactions in every state and province/territory- more than any single inspector, mortgage broker, title company, or insurance agency throughout the U.S. and Canada- and throughout those transactions and that more than 13 years of experience I can tell you with absolute certainty that an insanely high percentage of real estate agents treat every single deal as if they were buying the house for themselves.

Those are the facts, *whether you want to accept them or not is up to you*.

Public opinion is on my side here as well. In a Gallup poll in 2011, when respondents were asked if the ethical standards of people in a number of different fields were very high, high, average, low, or very low, 70% of respondents gave real estate agents average or above. In fact, they ranked higher than attorneys. They were ranked higher than stockbrokers. They were ranked higher than insurance salesmen, senators, governors, labor union leaders, and business executives.

Let's do a little math here to assess the value of the opinion of an inspector in the category of "Agent Hater." One of those inspectors who chooses to take the path of most resistance on a daily basis and be at war with the agents who refer better than 80% of the inspection business that happens throughout North America.

Let's say the inspector is average, which might be a generous assumption considering his disdain for the best referral source in the home inspection business, but let's say he does in fact book and complete 200 inspections annually.

Let's say 50% of those homes, once again being generous, had a significant structural issue, the kind agents supposedly don't want to hear anything about.

That's 100 inspections.

Let's now say that half of those, 50 inspections in total, had a buyer's agent present at them that actually approached the inspector in the way it gets told on forums and at chapter meetings, usually starting with, "You won't believe what this agent said to me..."

Fifty inspections.

Let's say they're in a market like Indianapolis with 20,000 transactions that happen every year. That comes out to ¼ of 1%.

If you made ¼ of 1% on a stock, would you get on the phone and start telling all your friends about it? Would you assume your stockbroker was a genius and invest your entire retirement fund with him and tell him to go to town?

Or maybe it's better to ask it this way, if you *lost* ¼ of 1% on a stock that your stockbroker had suggested, would you make sure everyone knew how bad he was and how no one should ever talk to him ever?

This phenomenon in the home inspection industry of small-time inspectors demonizing the entire real estate industry over their random, exceptional situations is unlike anything you'll find in any other industry.

What's more likely going on is that these inspectors who seem to run into a real estate agent who hates them everywhere they turn, probably didn't have the finesse they needed when they first got into the business. As a result, they had some bad experiences and have been fighting the war ever since.

It's sad really.

If this sounds like you, I am truly and sincerely sorry. I want to help you and I hope to accomplish this in two paragraphs.

In my experience, the bigger the inspection company, the less disdain and mistrust they have for real estate agents, which is good news for you. This means that the more transactions you do, the smaller the sampling of over-aggressive agents you might run into. That's hope for the future right there.

Regardless, let's say that agents truly do have it in for inspectors. *They are your referral source.* Put on a smile, play nice, and learn to get along with them. If that doesn't work, find an agent willing to let you shadow him for a week. After a week of living in their shoes, I promise you will have a better understanding of where they are coming from.

That is truly the key: *Understanding*.

It goes both ways. If you accept an education from an agent about what they deal with every day, they'll look forward to hearing the same from you. We're all on the same team, making sure the transaction is completed with accuracy and on fair terms for all parties.

If you are *truly* a good inspector, and you feel that any buyer in your marketplace would be well-served by having you as their home inspector, then stop being a hypocrite and do what it takes to represent more buyers. That means understanding the real estate business in its entirety, not just what you want to see in your little bubble.

If you have someone in your market that is the stereotypical "Agent Hater," take full advantage of that.

They are doing your marketing for you every time they open their mouths. Some of them even have Websites telling one-sided stories of unethical agents. Agents in your area deserve to know who the "deal killers" are, and the pitch goes something like this;

"I'm a home inspector, but I'm also a part of your team and we're working for the same people with the same goal in mind. Not every home I inspect is perfect, in fact almost none of them are, but there's almost nothing that can't be fixed and I find it easier to approach issues both major and minor calmly and professionally. Unfortunately, there are some in my profession who see things differently and pretty much start the relationship with your client in an alarmist made, at times even attempting to distance your client from their advisor in the transaction, you. I'm here to understand how I can do my job well while at the same time making your job easier, and I look forward to being a part of your team."

Make no mistake about it. Don Thornberry wanted the inspection company to find anything that they should. Give him a problem, he'll fix it. Like most agents, he will give you the opportunity to borrow his clients for a few hours if you have a solid reputation, but return them with undue anxiety and fear over a perfectly repairable issue, and you won't be hearing from any of his clients ever again.

A thorough inspection does not equate to an inspection that agents don't like, as much as some inspectors would like you to think is the case. An inspector with the personality and charm of sandpaper is what agents don't like, and if they don't like you that's why. Fix it.

Chapter 12
How to Install a Toilet

The coolest guy in the home inspection business is Jeff Donaldson. You may not know who I'm talking about, so let me tell you about Jeff. He is the owner of a multi-inspector firm in Charleston, South Carolina, and he's got a business that is kicking everybody's butt in his market.

Besides being a home inspector, he's also an Engineer, and he's got a program for inspectors that allow them to offer certain Engineering services that you'll find in the resources section of this book. It's called "My Engineer On Call."

All that makes him successful and a good guy to know if you're a home inspector, but what makes him cool is this:

He's one of the few people in the world who handled nuclear weapons.

If we had been put in the position of shooting one into Russia, he would have potentially been the guy to push the button from the nuclear-powered submarine he worked on in the Navy, or at least he would have been standing pretty close to the guy who did.

That's pretty cool.

It's surprising how humble he is about this experience, like it's no big deal. He was a mile below the ocean's surface in a nuclear powered submarine filled with enough firepower to wipe out a good part of the earth's population if aimed at the right spot, and it's no big deal to him. *I may have exaggerated on the "mile below the surface" part, and Jeff would probably say the reactor was really a lot more interesting than the weapons, but for all of us non-engineer civilians the whole thing is like a movie.*

If I ever do anything half that cool, you will all know it. This might be the reason the U.S. Department of Defense entrusted Jeff with nuclear materials and not me.

Perhaps if this part of Jeff's biography were in the program for the 2011 ASHI Inspection World in Phoenix, he would have had more than the 50-75 inspectors he did have in the course he taught.

Instead of taking Jeff's course on marketing lessons he had learned in his business, the majority of inspectors headed down the hall to the larger room where they were teaching a course on proper toilet installation.

I actually don't know if it was a course on toilet installation. It may have been, but if it wasn't it may as well have been.

Inspectors in Jeff's course got quite a treat. He gave them twenty or more things that he does in his business that have given his business the boost that took him from one inspector to four or five in a mid-level market like Charleston. He's in the top ½% of inspection companies by volume nationwide and he wasn't there to sell anything, only to pass on his knowledge to others seeking it.

I went to watch for a few minutes, and I was pleasantly surprised when he touched on RecallChek, 90-Day

Warranties, and even the ISG Call Center. Come to think of it, I still owe him a steak dinner.

He talked about all sorts of other things as well. Things that like RecallChek and 90-Day Warranties work and get him more referrals from real estate agents and past clients every day.

Going to seminars and conferences is important and technical courses are important. Courses that teach marketing and business practices are equally, if not more, important to most inspectors, so take a look at the courses and pick at least two business courses at every conference you go to. It's a sure-fire way to get out of the conference at least what you put into it in the way of airfare, hotel stays, admission fees, etc.

I'm proud of what ASHI has done over the last several years in the way of business courses. They've really stepped it up. Inspection World Phoenix was one of my favorite conferences of all time.

Let me give you my top ten conferences in no particular order:

1. Inspection World Phoenix

2. Casey O'Malley Vegas

3. Southeastern Conference

4. InterNACHI Florida

5. NAHI Annual Conference

6. Casey O'Malley Atlantic City

7. Pro-ASHI (Pittsburgh)

8. CREIA

9. Great Lakes ASHI Chapter

10. FABI

If you go to any of these conferences seeking some advice on growing your business, you'll find it in the form of courses as well as a vendor hall full of the top vendors in the industry ready to demonstrate what they can do for your business.

If you don't belong to more than one of the groups listed above, join. Go to at least two conferences every year with different groups. It's what the most successful inspectors in the business do. I can tell you from being at more than fifty conferences a year that anyone in Florida would benefit from going to NAHI's conference even if they attend every FABI meeting. Inspectors in Pittsburgh who go to every Pro-ASHI meeting would gain incredible insight by attending a CREIA conference.

Many of the inspectors I work with belong to ASHI, NAHI, and InterNACHI- and why not? What is the real cost of getting the information other inspectors in your market are getting from their associations as well as your own? A small membership fee every year. That's it.

I get that InterNACHI is the biggest, ASHI is the oldest, NAHI has some incredible benefits, and some of the state organizations are more specific to local needs. I know some of these organizations take issue with some of the others, but I don't care and you shouldn't either. You need to do what's best for *YOUR* business. That means getting everything you can from every available resource, and getting your technical requirements out of the way quickly to make room for the business and marketing aspects of what some of these organizations provide.

After all, there's only so much to learn about toilet installation.

Chapter 13
Pricing Yourself out of the Market

The latest cycle of ratings from the American Customer Satisfaction Index resulted in a list of *The 15 Most Disliked Companies in America*. Amongst the fifteen, four of them were airlines.

United, Delta, U S Airways, and American Airlines all made the list.

If it had been a list of the 25 or 30 most disliked companies, every major carrier would have most likely made the list. When my wife called me and told me about this list as it popped up on her Yahoo! home page, I told her to send me a link. Then I asked, "How many airlines made the list?"

"Why do you ask?" she said.

I knew they would be on there. Not because they want people to be unhappy, but because of the airline industry and the environment in which they operate.

If you have to ask why people hate the airlines, you must fly as little as my wife does. Ask anyone who flies frequently, they'll rattle off a list of issues.

Small, uncomfortable seating, inefficient boarding methods, delays, not doing enough for their passengers when there are delays, dated planes without televisions and Wi-Fi, not enough direct flights, fees for baggage, fees for sitting in an exit row, minimal level of service, and the cost to fly is too high and inconsistent.

The only airline I *knew* wouldn't be on that list was Southwest. Why? Southwest is the only airline with a different business model. They book many of their flights on their own Website, they don't assign seats, you don't have to wait for first class to board before you do, and they don't charge for baggage.

Oh, and every Southwest plane is the same, a 737. That means their crews are all trained for every plane in the fleet, and delays due to staffing are incredibly infrequent. Plus their maintenance guys only have to work on one type of aircraft and they only have to stock parts for 737's.

There's a lot to be said for having something that makes your business unique, it can help you overcome incredible challenges like the primary reason the airlines end up at the top of the most hated list, pricing.

Airlines have taken fare models to the extreme with their availability-based pricing. Every time a seat is booked on an airplane, the price changes for all remaining available seats. Booking at the last minute is going to be incredibly expensive if there are only a couple of seats left.

Next time you're on a plane, ask the person next to you how much they paid. It could be half of what you paid or it could be double or triple. The airlines charge as much as they possibly can for every seat on an airplane and they're proud of it.

I believe that most inspectors charge too little. Not for what they're offering, but for what they should be offering. Add some benefits to your inspection, increase your fee, but don't go crazy.

I know of a couple of inspectors in different parts of the country who tried the "pricing on availability" model...and it hurt their business badly.

Even in a multi-inspector environment, managing such a pricing structure is messy. Even if you master the management of the pricing, you're still going to run into the problem of your inconsistent pricing turning off agents and clients alike.

As it turns out, agents like consistency. They *really* don't like it when they refer a client to your company and they get a price that is so far out of line with everyone else that it makes them look bad for strongly recommending you.

While these inspectors had a great concept when it came to implementing a progressive pricing structure and I applaud them for creativity, in practice it did nothing but lose them referral sources gradually throughout the busy season so badly that by the fall the availability pricing system had cost them huge amounts of money. Many times over what they made by charging a few home buyers basically whatever they were willing to spend during the busiest months.

It's not just the pricing method that can lose you customers. The pricing itself can be a problem.

I know quite a few inspectors who charged what I would call exorbitant fees for inspections at one point or another, and usually started doing so in a great market. Not just high prices, but incredibly high prices.

It worked for them for a month or two, maybe even a year...but the idea that they could do fewer inspections for massive profits turned out to be short-lived as once again the rule that agents don't appreciate looking bad took hold.

When all of your competition is at or below $500 for their base inspection fee in your area, and you're at $1500, at some point you're going to lose the business. It's that simple.

All it takes is one dinner conversation between your client and a friend of his who spent 1/3rd of what your client did and conceivably ended up with the same results, and they are calling their agent to ask them why they had to pay so much.

The agent may love you, he may be your biggest fan, but he can only defend your price structure to so many clients before he has to figure out another way to do business and may not even call you to tell you why you're off the list.

Airlines can get away with this. There are only so many choices and they're all similarly priced to begin with- Inspectors not so much.

The best thing to do to maximize profitability is to figure out whether or not you're going to go multi-inspector or remain a single inspector firm. Then you can approach the pricing dilemma intelligently.

Let's start with single inspectors who have no intention of ever being a multi-inspector firm. Maybe you don't want to manage people, maybe your market isn't big enough to support multiple inspectors, whatever your reason I understand completely.

So let's figure out what hours you want to work, how many days you want to work, and how many inspections you can do comfortably in that time period.

Maybe it's two per day, five days per week for a total of ten inspections per week, with two weeks off each year, for a total of 500 inspections.

Now go pick up a rock, throw it thirty feet in any direction, and you will find someone who will at this juncture give you very bad advice. They're everywhere...people who believe they are giving you good advice by telling you to raise your prices. They'll point to an equation where a Website or a book somewhere shows that reducing your price by 30% makes it so you have to sell 66% more product to make the same profit and that by simply raising your price by 10% you increase profitability by 25% or some other nonsense that's based on manufacturing a widget and then selling it out of a store that has ridiculously low overhead.

These people know nothing of the home inspection business. They really don't know that much about business at all. Parrots have the ability to repeat in the same way they do.

Let's actually come up with a solution to deliver you maximum profitability and consistent pay. The kind of business you'd like to have for your own sanity.

The key to raising prices is not doing it initially, but rather once you have volume. Raising your price $20 on 100 inspections is a total of $2,000. Raising your price $20 on 500 inspections is $10,000. Which one would you rather have?

Of course the answer is the larger of the two, so the key is having that volume of business to raise the rate on. That means inspections coming in at the rate you need to in order to make business come your way- profitably.

In other words, figure out your basis (cost of doing an inspection) and price your inspections above that but below the highest prices in the area in order to give your marketing message the best chance at success in acquiring new referral sources, also known as real estate agents.

Maybe you do 100 inspections this year, and maybe 200 next year. Don't make a substantial move in pricing. Keep building the number of inspections, and be patient.

Keep marketing, add to your services, make your company unique. Keep your referral sources happy and get your volume up toward 400 per year.

Now raise your price a bit, and make sure the business remains stable. Raise it a bit more, but keep in line with competitors to some extent.

Now go back out and market yourself with the higher fee schedule, and see if you can fill the rest of your schedule without too much difficulty.

If bringing on new clients to replace any lost referral sources proves either very difficult or impossible, you've hit a price point that your current marketing message cannot support. It's not a debatable point- it's absolute.

That doesn't mean your prices retreat. If you've managed to keep the original volume you built up and your referral sources remain loyal, you just need to change your offering.

Add some USP's. Do some sales meetings and educational sessions for agents. Hire a marketing representative to get your message in front of more agents.

Eventually you're going to find the balance where you're making a very good profit on each inspection while also refraining from tying a pricing noose around your business and making it impossible to acquire new referral sources to replace those that leave the business or go elsewhere for whatever reason.

For those looking to become a multi-inspector firm, the pricing puzzle becomes a great deal more complicated. It's part of a much bigger topic as well: The Multi-Inspector Mindset.

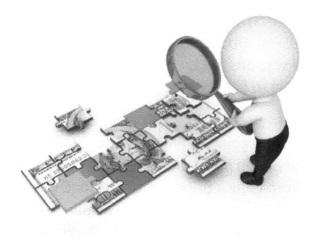

Chapter 14
The Multi-Inspector Mindset

In the early 80's when Security Home Inspections was founded, there wasn't an Internet. There weren't inspector training schools like there are today.

Phil & Patty Thornberry had no idea what a home inspection company was supposed to look like, and there were few competitors. The one right down the street was Surette & Associates, owned by Dave Surette. He had multiple inspectors and ran the business out of a house that had been converted into an office. He had three sons who eventually got into the family business, and when the time was right he passed on the torch and went on to found RAL, the company that sources the lion's share of relocation inspections throughout the U.S.

Dave Surette had office staff answering the phone and did a pretty decent job of branding his business. I'm not sure how much Dave influenced the way my parents conducted their business in the early days, but it seems hardly coincidental that they did everything they needed to in order to get that first office...about a quarter mile away from Dave's and on the same street (Now a burger joint called "Bub's"). Dave and Phil would often see each other in the morning at the post office, with incoming mailboxes on the same wall.

Phil and Patty Thornberry took the brand name of Phil's electrical contracting business (Security Electric) and Patty's knowledge of the real estate transaction, and went to town building what would become one of the largest inspection companies ever. You can't do that without multiple inspectors to cover demand when you get ten, twenty, or even fifty plus orders per day.

It was common sense to them that the limiting factor to home inspection growth was capacity.

This is the defining characteristic of someone who has the multi-inspector mindset. They look at the business model and go into it wanting to serve as many clients as possible, being involved in as many real estate transactions as possible, and creating jobs through expansion.

Profit is certainly a consideration, but it's almost secondary.

For the inspector with the multi-inspector mindset, the goal of being the biggest and the best is much more exciting than making the most money off any single home inspection. It's the thrill of growth, getting more business, and being more competitive than anyone else in the market.

The single-inspector mindset is much more subdued- it focuses primarily on the inspection process itself. Some will even get to the point that hiring another inspector might be a good business decision, but they don't. They might be concerned that the next guy will be a liability or won't be as good as *they* are at inspecting. They may just not want to manage people, and that's a perfectly respectable position.

I'm the opposite. I want hundreds of employees, offices in every major city, and a brand that is recognizable coast to coast.

You could tell me that I would be happier, even perhaps wealthier, with a medium-sized company with a staff of less than twenty, but I wouldn't be interested. That sounds boring.

If you're the same way, you've got the multi-inspector mindset. If you don't, there's nothing wrong with you and no book will change who you are. Read the rest of this book five times and skip this chapter. Come back if something changes.

There's nothing more important than doing things your way, and being happy about it. Your way may include not having employees, and that's perfectly fine.

Now let's examine the structural changes you'll need to make in order to be successful as a multi-inspector firm.

If the name of your inspection company includes your first or last name or both, you need to seriously consider making a change. As a multi-inspector firm, you need to be able to schedule inspections with your staff. If your name is on the door, people are going to want you and they'll potentially feel cheated if they don't get you. It might be painful, but the longer you wait the more painful it is. You may be able to use the name you have but convert it to an acronym. For instance, if your company is called "P. Nathan Thornberry Inspections," you could very easily transition to "PNT *Professional Inspections.*"

Now that the name is determined, clients absolutely need to get the sense that when they call you they are dealing with an enterprise. If your cell phone is your company phone number, change it. If you personally answer every phone call, get a call center.

If you're going to build a big inspection business, it can't be based on your personality or personal ability to sell your service. You need to create a system for taking orders, and either place that in the hands of a call center or hire an office administrator to handle the calls. If the system doesn't work, fix it.

At any given time at Security Home Inspections, ten phone lines can light up and eight of those calls might be orders. Calling people back is not an option. The staff is in place; they're all perfectly qualified to take an order. Will they do it as well as Phil or Patty Thornberry the owners, himself or herself? Probably not, but the business is not Phil & Patty. It's Security Home Inspections.

In one page, we've addressed most of the structural issues from a business operations perspective.

Now comes the painful part for most inspectors.

Is your inspection process efficient and duplicative?

From the process of inspecting itself, to filling out reports and delivering them, is the process something that could be learned by someone with basic home inspection training in a period of 90 days?

The immediate response you just had in your head is very telling. Maybe you thought to yourself, "Yes!" If that's the case, it should be smooth sailing. If the answer was either "No," "Not Really," or "Umm..." then we have a problem.

How many 1,500 square foot home inspections can you do in a day?

If it's two or three (preferably three), this is going to be easy for you.

If it's one, you have a problem. A serious problem.

If your goal were to be a single man operation, the answers to these questions wouldn't really matter much. If you're personally comfortable with what you do, great, but as soon as you start hiring staff and you have committed to keeping them busy, one inspection per day just doesn't cut it.

Your inspection needs to have plenty of comments ready to go, and it needs to come out of a system that's easy to use and scalable to any number of inspectors. You need to seek out someone in the inspection software industry who has experience in this- like Carl Fowler with 3-D or Dominic Maricic of Home Inspector Pro or John Kwasnik of Horizon. I've listed some others as well in the resources section of this book, but these three I have personal experience with specifically implementing multi-inspector firms.

Don't worry so much about the process until you get the report down, because a good, easy to use report can help you greatly in defining a process for your future inspectors.

Stay away from software that doesn't allow you to brand yourself exclusively. This is extremely important. You need to brand yourself. When you brand someone else, clients can very easily find a smaller competitor with the same system and think, "They're the same, only cheaper."

This is something you want to avoid.

Likewise, there are newsletter services out there, free Websites, all sorts of resources that would be fine if only they focused on *YOUR* brand.

This is just one area where it's worth mentioning that The Inspector Services Group really meets your need to brand yourself. Everything we do is branded with the inspector's logo and we ensure the inspector gets credit for everything (or the agent who referred him, whichever makes sense).

Which brings us back to the pricing models we covered in the last chapter. With a multi-inspector firm, pricing becomes an incredibly complicated labyrinth.

You really have to take into consideration so many factors that a simple equation to follow just doesn't exist. To some extent, you are limited by supply and demand and prevailing rates, but at the same time a well-branded multi-inspector firm can become a trailblazer when it comes to setting inspection standards and pricing as well.

In the resources section, you'll find a section regarding pricing for multi-inspector firms. It would be a good idea to check that out.

Running a multi-inspector firm is much more about running a business than it is about home inspecting. If you decide to go down that path, it will be stressful at times, but incredibly rewarding.

Chapter 15
SOPs are so Twenty Years Ago

The various Standards of Practice that exist today from the major inspection organizations as well as the state licensing agencies are by and large good. There's nothing inherently wrong with having a minimum standard for an industry.

SOPs offer two specific benefits to home inspectors:

1. They make public a set of minimum standards, giving credibility to membership in an association or licensure.

2. They set parameters for inspections as general guidelines to prevent us having to "reinvent the wheel."

If we didn't have standards, both in ethical matters and in how we inspect, our industry would likely not have the credibility it does in the public eye. Some believe that the SOPs are liability protection and they are not. The only reason they serve to reduce our liability is that they give us minimum guidelines within which to operate, and prevent inspectors from doing lower-grade inspections that would not include the basics.

The exception to that would be if the standards are included or referenced in your inspection contract, at which point they become the definition of your scope of inspection. In that case, yes the SOPs serve as a limited layer of liability protection. I say "limited" because I've met a few judges and I've yet to meet one who takes the time to read the SOPs or acknowledges them in any meaningful way. The SOPs aren't inherently something a consumer is mindful of, and usually the contractor's opinion of the defect and whether it was "noticeable" gets asked. That's what the judge goes by much more than a standard you put forth that he's never heard of, is not going to read, and doesn't really care about because he's looking for *you* to show how you did not damage the other party. Was it "unavoidable" or outside of your control? Are you leaning on these standards as an excuse for negligence? I know, it's hardly fair, but it's reality.

The other reason I say SOPs provide very "limited" liability protection is because lawsuits and errors & omissions claims rarely come about as a result of an inspector *exceeding* the minimum standards and finding problems they would have otherwise missed or had no obligation to find in the first place. Claims and lawsuits are more likely the result of bad communication, frivolous/crazy clients out to cost someone money, the inspector not meeting the minimum standard in the first place, or rather, missing something he should have caught while performing an inspection up to those minimum standards.

Outside of the debate as to whether the standards are good and whether or not they protect inspectors, the SOPs are most often misused.

They get misused by inspectors who are stuck in the past, twenty years ago or more, as an excuse for the fact that they (the inspectors) are becoming irrelevant.

Let me give you an example;

I know that checking for recalls isn't a part of the minimum standard. It's up to an inspector to decide if they want to check for recalls as part of their inspection and offer superior service to their clients. I personally believe that checking for recalls will eventually become a standard, and I think it's silly that we argue about how far an inspector's head should go into the corner of an attic and don't acknowledge as an industry that one in every ten homes he inspected in the last year had a known fire hazard right there in the kitchen staring him in the face. The solution was simple, it was available for free, and it's from a major sponsor of every association and inspector event everywhere, and it's *RecallChek*.

For now, it remains beyond the standard and I like that it's considered a "premium" service. It's giving inspectors an edge in their market and making them more successful.

In one major market out west, I have three incredibly competitive multi-inspector firms offering RecallChek with every inspection, and about 30 smaller (what we call "big companies in development") firms doing the same. I've visited there, done presentations to real estate offices, and in every resource area in those real estate offices I found colorful, well done fliers from inspectors who focused on USPs like RecallChek, 90-Day Warranties, and even our Termite Protection Plans.

I say all this because there is an inspector in this market whom I've known for many years, and while he was never a client I thought we were on very good terms. Until one day I was at an inspector conference, sponsoring the event, and he came up to me and asked how things are going.

I say, "Never been better!"

I was having a good show, probably 30% of the attendees had already signed up for *RecallChek*, which he had noticed, and it bugged the heck out of him.

You see, this inspector, we'll call him Manwich just to avoid using anyone's name, has been inspecting for decades. He's been in leadership positions in a major association, he's known the guys on the committees that come up with the standards for years and years...and Manwich is the kind of inspector who uses the SOPs in the wrong way.

When a client calls Manwich to get a price, and they ask if he uses an IR camera, if he checks for recalls, if he offers a warranty, or asks any other question about his services that go beyond the bare minimum required by the association's SOPs that he subscribes to, the answer is a very bitter, "No, that's not a part of our standards." He goes on to insult the other companies to the prospective client, which ultimately results in him not getting the order, and he's losing a *lot* of business to the competition.

His business is no longer about the customer, it's no longer about having fun doing what you do, it has become a losing battle.

Every time I see him at a convention, the clients who choose someone else after asking him a question he's uncomfortable with become more and more frequent.

Don't get me wrong, it's not just *RecallChek* or 90-Day Warranties and it's certainly not my personal influence exclusively causing these problems for him. The companies I deal with in his area are creative and competitive and they're coming up with new ways to get business all the time.

I'm just the most noticeable cause of his problems.

What I had been mistaking for an inviting humor-filled smirk all these years was actually a disdainful, "you jerk" kind of look. I had no idea! I think I handled his venting pretty well, but he refused to take any responsibility for his own failures. He actually suggested that he had the influence to change the SOP in such a way that inspectors would not be allowed to go beyond it.

I suggested why he was at it to go ahead and set the pricing for the industry as well. I was being sarcastic, but apparently that is also an issue for him.

Don't be a Manwich. The SOP is a minimum standard. What really matters is what clients want and what will make you appealing as a company to hire for a home inspection. I'm pretty sure you can pass high school with a D- and do only the required activities every day- I just never thought to try.

Stay *hungry* my friends.

Chapter 16
Contributions

If you've ever heard the phrase "eating your own dog food," you know that you can't trust the advice of someone who doesn't do what they are telling you that you should do.

Developing strong partnerships and relationships throughout the industry is crucial to our business, and not only do I rely on several people and organizations to help me promote my business, but I endorse theirs as well. We are affiliate members of any organization you've ever heard of- ASHI, NAHI, InterNACHI, CREIA, FABI, CAHPI, and everything in between- and I suggest you get as much information as you can from multiple associations but also tap the resources you'll find in the vendor hall and in this book. *Any one of the* contributors to this book (mostly vendors) have a great deal to offer you- and that doesn't mean you have to buy anything necessarily.

Just talk to them.

When I sent out an email to the industry's leading vendors, I asked if they would put down on paper a few things that might help an inspectors business. *The response was amazing.*

There were a few people that I couldn't get into the final version of the book, so let take a page or two to thank everyone that has helped me and thousands of inspectors, and tell you why I like them.

Bob Pearson (Allen Insurance) does more for the home inspection industry than you might realize, and if you have errors and omissions insurance, there's a good chance it's with him. If your insurance isn't with Bob, there's no doubt that your policy has been modeled in some way after something he has done.

Carl Fowler (3-D Software) made the inspection reporting software business what it is today, and continues to be the leader in the inspection software business. Carl and his lead programmer, Charles, were the first report software company to incorporate into their programming our *RecallChek* integration module- which may or may not have affected you, but it speaks to their commitment to the industry and making your jobs easier.

Dan Steward (Pillar to Post) and Lenny Rankin (HouseMaster) are two of the true executives in the home inspection industry. I've nothing but good things to say about most franchise systems, but these guys are phenomenal managers delivering value to their franchisees every day. It would be impossible to mention either one of these gentlemen without saying a word about Kathleen Kuhn (HouseMaster) and everything she did for the entire industry through promotion and media coverage.

Russ Colliau (IMS) showed me how to run a webinar- and after the first one I was hooked! I've seen him take an hour or even longer counseling an individual inspector (who wasn't even a client by the way) on some troubles he was having in his business. He's probably one of the more exciting people you'll ever talk to. His business is automation, and you'll find more about IMS in the resources section at the end of this chapter.

Dominic Maricic (Home Inspector Pro) is a teacher. He may sell you some inspection software or perhaps web hosting, but at his core he is a teacher and you can learn a lot from him- as many inspectors have. If your presence on the web is lacking, it's "Dom" you should be asking.

Mike Crow (Millionaire Inspector Community) is the industry's leading business coach and the very basic concept he instills in his members most is being unique- it has been the basis for many of the elements we've built into our products and the one thing that has contributed most to our success.

Alan Carson (Carson Dunlop/Horizon Software) is a true home inspection innovator. John Kwasnik is the go-to guy at his Horizon software company that offers the only combination scheduling and reporting package you should consider.

Dan Huber (ISN) and Chris Schuld help inspectors automate their businesses and their marketing, and I've come to have great respect for the way they operate. You can learn a lot about customer service from them, and how to establish excellent communication.

Terry Howell (Radalink) is the expert you need to talk to about Radon testing. His Radalink monitors are more than just Radon testing equipment- they are part of a Radon system that saves inspectors time and money and deliver the highest level of professional reports to clients.

Hollis Brown (YadZooks) is inexplicably helpful. To everyone. His online solutions and applications are incredibly cheap (or free) and his network of linked inspection companies is probably the largest in the world.

Paul Zak (America's Call Center) is the office manager for inspection companies all over the U.S. If you're looking for your clients to have an exceptional experience when they call your "office," Paul can deliver that.

Nick Gromicko (founder, InterNACHI) is probably one of the most brilliant marketers in the industry- love him or hate him, you can't deny that! He's built the largest organization of inspectors and taken it to international status. *He is NOT someone to be ignored.*

Jeff Donaldson (My Engineer on Call) is an Engineer and owner of a multi-inspector firm in Charleston, South Carolina. He was one of our first *RecallChek* users and his My Engineer on Call system is truly revolutionary.

Mike Casey and Kevin O'Malley (Casey O'Malley Associates) have trained a good portion of this industry to become inspectors in the first place- and continue to be the source for education. If you haven't been to their Las Vegas or Atlantic City shows, you're missing out!

Special thanks as well to the leadership of CREIA, for allowing me the honor of being the first vendor ever to speak at leadership day. Thanks to Bill Lewis and the staff at ASHI for all their hard work and the improvements they've made to their events over the years and for continuing to carry the torch they lit decades ago with such honor. Thanks to NAHI for putting together a marketing day preceding their annual convention and having the foresight to inject a marketing mindset into their membership.

And a very special thanks to those who have taught me more about this business over the years than I ever could have asked for- you know who you are- Hank R., Bob M., Dennis H., Liz R., Patty & Phil, Brian A., Darryl J., Arvil P., Preston S., Paul & Sharon, Gordon F., Chad H., Tim M., Rob & Michelle, Donna J., Donna & Jamie, Dawn H., Joe M., Randy S., Tony S., Tony C., Frank, Phil L., Michelle & Greg, Wally & Tonya, Al R., John V., Don S., my Friends at GLC, the whole community at MIC, Alan and the rest of the Executives, Steve & Pat and the rest of the WIN family, Roland & Bill at NPI/GPI, Kal Patel, and our friends at HomeTeam.

Needless to say, there are plenty of other significant people in the industry that I should mention...but this book can only be so long!

Without further ado...let's find out what the experts in the industry with over 200 years combined experience have to say about achieving success in home inspection.

Contributing Authors

Reality Check

by Bob Pearson

Allen Insurance

I have had the privilege to talk to/work with more inspectors than probably any one individual in our industry. Along the way, I've offered policies that appeal to seasoned veterans and policies that appeal to new inspectors where they pay "per inspection." What did I learn? It was shocking...

Only 5% of new inspectors are still in business at the end of their first year – absolutely great technicians but no marketing skills. They didn't necessarily have higher claims for the number of inspections they did, they just didn't have orders.

Getting those first orders and then establishing a referral base is important. I hope you take it to the next level.

I believe I have attended every annual meeting Mike Crow has ever put on and I try to sit in for at least some of Dominic Maricic's presentations when I can – and I always learn something new that helps in my business. If you do a Google search for "Home Inspector Insurance" I always come up first and I do not pay for it! – thanks Dominic!

Beyond the web though, there's an absolute need for real and evident sales efforts in your local market. I've worked with several large inspection companies and all of them had one thing in common- a marketing rep (at least one).

Regardless of whether you want to be a multi-inspector firm, or just go at it alone (and both are perfectly respectable by the way), if you're a professional try to look like one.

Wear a uniform.

Answer your phones.

I would say 75-80% of the inspectors I work with regularly allow calls to go to voicemail. Those would be the *bottom* 75-80% of inspectors I work with (by volume).

Just a few thoughts from the gray-haired guy in the back of the room.

Franchises Make Sense for Many- *Even Veteran Home Inspectors*

By Dan Steward

Pillar to Post

The home inspection industry continues to mature and evolve and there are multiple ways that one can make a nice living in the business. The origins of the industry lay in the tradesman turned advisor. Now the independent, owner-operator inspector makes up most of the industry. However the multi-inspector and the branded franchise business model are rapidly gaining market significance.

The franchise model has existed for about 25 years and gained rapid growth in the late '90s and early 2000s. Companies such as Pillar To Post, Amerispec, HouseMaster and WIN have lead the way in advancing the branded franchise model. In some ways the franchise model can be characterized as being in business "for yourself" but not "by yourself".

The history of the real estate business over the last two or three decades may provide some indication of the future for the home inspections business. While there continues to be many good and successful private real estate brokerage firms, a great portion of all real estate transactions are now done through the branded franchise real estate brokerage such as RE/MAX, Keller Williams, Coldwell Banker and so on. The consumer's desire and need for confidence, the increasing complexity of the industry, increased need for technology and ongoing education, the need for support for the front line practitioner, the need for powerful and effective marketing have all contributed to changing the face of the real estate brokerage business away from independents and toward strong franchise brands in recent years.

These same consumer preferences and demands will strongly influence the shift in the home inspection industry to a greater role and market share for the strong franchise brands and for those independents that do an excellent job of presenting their brand as something bigger than a single inspector operation.

Standards established and exercised by professional franchise brands have been proven sources of trust for consumers and business opportunity for franchisees- and they pave the way for independents as well.

For business owners, the franchise model has brought significant benefits. Given the failure rate of new independent businesses or the inability of those businesses to build adequate income and wealth for their owner, the franchise model brings higher certainty for the unit owner.

The home inspection industry is evolving rapidly, long past the tradesman turned advisor days. Our foundation stills lies solidly in understanding building science. Increasingly however, other factors are becoming significant demands on an inspector as requirements for success.

- Consumers – at the heart of the home inspection business is the home buyer (generally) who is looking for information, education and peace of mind. As the cost of housing increases, the homes gets older, major systems become more complex and consumers become better educated and more demanding, the "clip board and flashlight" home inspector is no longer a viable service.

• Real estate agents and brokers – while the history of the relationship between home inspectors and real estate agents may have been a mixed one, today's home inspection is an ingrained part of the vast majority of resale transactions. Professional REALTORS want to deliver a great experience for their clients and a great home inspection experience is part of that. They too want predictability, reliability, quality and ready availability from their home inspectors. The old marketing expression that "loyalty is just the absence of a better offer" could apply to the real estate agent relationship. They rightly expect quality, integrity, current knowledge and technology to help them succeed in their role.

• Marketing – otherwise known as the acquisition, retention and management of customers is increasingly complex and challenging. The independent home inspector is faced with extraordinary demands ranging from using Facebook, LinkedIn, Twitter, and blogs to communicate outwardly, to keeping a fresh and active website, to deciding on office sponsorships, media advertising and so on. There are countless ways to spend (or blow away) marketing dollars and time. Acquiring and caring for new customers, be they real estate agents or consumers, is an essential everyday matter for an inspection business to succeed.

- Technology – how many inspectors have been intrigued by cool new bright shiny toys, such as infrared cameras to name one example? Technology is a two sided matter. The first being how do you keep current with what's available, learn it and build it into your business? This could be infrared, or computerized reporting or indoor air quality assessments and so on. You only have to attend one industry conference to see the overwhelming offerings of new business and service technologies. The other side of the technology matter is how you generate a return on the investment in that technology. The often recited comment from the IR manufacturers that IR is just the new standard and you have to have one is craziness. Home inspection is a business, a business to serve our customers and generate *PROFIT*!

- Wealth – If you are in business to build wealth, can you sell your business when you are ready? Independent, personal services businesses have little resale value given the dependence on the owner and lack of brand identity and operating systems. The resale value of branded franchises has been well proven- if you're on the independent side you need to dedicate significant resources to branding and systems if you plan on selling your business as an asset. Then there is the process of actually finding a suitable buyer- good franchisors help with the transfer process including helping to find a buyer, ultimately helping the operator realize the wealth from the business they have built. Business brokers can serve that purpose for independents but beware...it's a minefield.

Building a brand can be a lot of fun, but more and more even veteran inspectors are finding the franchise model appealing. It's a complex world, find advisors you can trust and keep in mind that several of them come in the form of the largest franchisors in the home inspection business.

Are you a Technician or Business Owner?

Carl Fowler

3-D

I've been an observer of the home inspection industry for many years, the first 20 as an active home inspector and the last 25 years as president of an inspection reporting Software Company. This put me in a unique position to be able to understand the inner workings of the home inspection business and to know and observe the cycle that many owners of home inspection businesses go through, from their beginnings in the business to their exit into retirement. I personally know some who sold their home inspection businesses for millions, and I have known many more that simply disconnected their phone.

The difference between the ones who sold for big bucks and the ones who simply stopped working comes down to one thing... Were they an expert inspector or a company?

The typical home inspection firm starts as a one person operation. This "single man operator" answers the phone, sells the job, schedules the jobs, does the inspections, writes the report, and handles all related follow up, including marketing.

As one successful inspection follows another, the inspector gets a bloated ego and becomes so busy being an expert that he forgets to build his business. The fact that he can net $50K-$70K per year keeps him on track for doing it the same way his entire life. Eventually he wears out and retires.

That's not the way it is in many other businesses. If you call a plumber or electrician or any other number of trades, the person who answers the phone is not usually the person who fixes your problem at any decent sized organization. They offer to send an employee to do the job. In the end the owner sells out to his employees or another firm.

The guy who wants to grow a business ultimately hires others to do inspections. His job description is no longer to be the best inspector he can, but to be the best manager of inspectors. Next he organizes the work processes and work flow, institutes an in-house training program and hires an office manager to relieve him even more. Finally he sets about doing what he should be doing, and that is marketing. That means joining the Chamber of Commerce, the local REALTOR boards and the like, speaking to them at every opportunity and even attending some of their social functions. He finds that's not such a bad job, being the ambassador for the business.

Yesterday's successful inspection business owners spent equal amounts of time being an ambassador, managing customers, and dealing with inspectors and their schedules. Gross income rose to the million mark and even higher in many cases; the opportunity to sell became possible.

Just like the internet made it possible for anyone to be in business, the release of cloud based reporting software in 2011 made it possible for anyone to grow an inspection organization easily.

The owner of the business now provides the functions of marketing, order capture and report review. The business owner hires someone to answer the phone, book new jobs and assigns them to inspectors based on their location. Remote inspectors receive their jobs via Android or Windows powered handheld devices of their choice, tablets, or phones. Employee inspectors can make their own schedules and then gather inspection data along with photographs in their handheld devices, and immediately upload them to the main office. The business owner then converts the report, reviews it and sends it out to the client. The employee inspector gets paid only for gathering the information, not writing the report, cutting down the time he would have invested in the job.

The business owner has several advantages. He controls the money. He controls the client. He controls the inspection wording and process via forms sent to inspectors. He controls inspectors and their reports more efficiently, as driving time is eliminated. He can devote more time to training and marketing, which builds his business further.

As I have seen so many times, single operator inspectors get so busy working in their business that they don't have time or energy *to work on the business*. Software available today can help you change the outcome of your business, if you are open to changing your ways.

Brutality Online

Nick Gromicko

InterNACHI

The home inspection business is different than almost any other business in that you (the home inspector) never meet your client until AFTER you're hired. When you get out of your truck at the inspection site and introduce yourself to your client, they have already hired you. There is almost no salesmanship involved in the home inspection business. Success relies almost solely on marketing.

Where then should an inspector market? Well, a home inspector's clients are nearly always home buyers. And many of these home buyers are conveniently all in one place... online. They are online touring new homes, researching schools, emailing their real estate agents, shopping for mortgages, and looking for home inspectors. And since you won't have an opportunity to sell your inspection services in person, it's important that your website be capable of doing your selling for you. To a potential client, your website is a sample of what you and your report are going to be like. It makes little sense to drive traffic to a website that doesn't represent you well. The door to your website is your homepage. It's the most important page of your website. Most of your visitors will never even click through to your other pages if your homepage doesn't make them want more. As a home inspector, you might work on some of the most expensive real estate in the world, but no home is as valuable, per square foot, as your own inspection website's homepage. The right homepage can generate you many thousands of dollars in inspection business, if it's designed properly. You only get one chance to make a good first impression. Make sure your site doesn't un-sell your inspection services.

For more on this topic, visit;

http://www.nachi.org/brutal.htm#ixzz215ulY784

I Have Never Gone Hungry

Jeff Donaldson

My Engineer on Call

There was a time I embraced many of the misconceptions that permeate our industry, and they held me back. It took a long time to shake the negativity out of my mind, but even now I still have occasional lapses that make me paranoid and overly defensive. I am thankful that I found the resources to help me overcome my limitations, stay focused on being successful, and assemble a true home inspection business.

I am a licensed professional engineer, which is somewhat of a rarity in the home inspection industry. You don't have to be an engineer to do a home inspection, but it certainly has its advantages when it comes to gaining credibility.

Although I have never used a pocket protector, I used to be much more like the stereotypical engineer – introverted, analytical, and a bit of a geek. I had to overcome these tendencies to be a successful home inspector, especially the introverted part. I'm still not a party animal, but I have learned what I need to do operate and promote my business. This took a lot of focused effort, but let me encourage you – you can overcome your limitations once you recognize them and want to change.

Long ago, I realized the value of offering myself as a resource whenever anyone has a question or problem involving inspections, construction or problems with a house. Over the years I have helped many agents, mortgage brokers and closing attorneys resolve challenges. In many cases the solution did not involve a billable sale or use of the services we offer. People remember, however, that I was willing and available to help and that has paid tremendous dividends over the years.

As my home inspection business has grown, I added inspectors who were not engineers, and the engineer's advantage I enjoyed began to turn into a liability. Everyone wanted "the engineer", but there were only so many hours in the day. Customers would go elsewhere when I was not available. I needed to find a solution, and fast.

So we started emphasizing that even though all of our inspectors were not engineers, they were all trained by an engineer- exhaustively, extensively, and continuously. Customers liked the explanation and we continued to grow, but we still lost a disturbing number of jobs. So, in addition to the emphasis on training, I offered a free engineering consultation – if the inspector identified a condition that needed an engineer's attention, I would personally review the matter with the customer to help them understand its significance and some basic repair strategies. Why not, I reasoned – I would do it anyway when they asked. Bingo – we were back in business!

All it took was offering clients something beyond what the competition was able or willing to offer. We added *RecallChek*, and we grew some more. Then we added the 90-Day Warranty.

Every time we add something to our services, clients choose us more often. There are dozens of things you can add into your service offering that will make you look more like a Hyatt Regency than a Super 8- and each one of them will impress not only your clients but also make those who referred them look good.

One of those things you might consider is engineering services- and yes, there *is a way* for you to offer them. From manufactured trusses and joists to laminated beams, with just a small amount of training you can gather data for an Engineer who can deliver the results your clients are looking for at a lower cost in most cases than having an Engineer do a site visit.

Zero to Hero

By Kevin O'Malley

Casey O'Mally Associates

Feel like you had it and now it is gone?

The game has changed, times are tough, life is hard, the economy sucks, real estate sales are down, etc., etc. Forget the past and prepare for your future.

I was asked to speak at an inspector association chapter meeting and they wanted me to talk about marketing. Well they were in luck because I love to talk business.

Many of the inspectors there had been my students in the past twenty-five years (Mike Casey and I have trained around 15,000 inspectors throughout the U.S.) and were now grumbling about the downturn in business. Most of the inspectors attending the talk would be considered veterans with ten or more years inspecting. A few were newbies. The vast majority had no significant plans in place to create new business.

The most interesting thing happened in the first fifteen minutes of the talk. I asked everyone in the audience to tell me one thing they did that past week that got them an inspection job that past week. Only one inspector in a group of about fifty inspectors could really pinpoint something they did that caused the phone to ring for work. The others were saying things like they did a thorough inspection, word of mouth and other non-tangible events.

It was amazing to think that these very good inspectors had been overlooking what to do about marketing their services. I then asked what they thought made them different or unique from the rest of their competition. This again was a big surprise with responses similar to the first question. They thought because they were thorough that made them special.

I have been preaching for years that the most important thing in your home inspection business is to have a unique selling proposition. Simply put, be different. This is important now more than ever. Sitting back and thinking that business as usual will produce the desired results is ludicrous. It will not. You must create a very appealing, unique product offering. Offer incredible benefits to your customers. Give more than expected. Make people wonder why other inspectors are not doing as much as you are.

Once you have a product you can sell, work on your marketing plan. When you are not inspecting you must be marketing.

I met P. Nathan Thornberry a number of years ago when I returned to the inspection training profession after a brief hiatus. He has created a number of products which will help inspectors create their unique selling propositions and stand out in the crowded inspector marketplace. Dominic Maricic is another individual to get to know. He has incredible knowledge that will help inspectors with today's online marketing needs and social networking skills. Just don't forget that you are in a trust and relationship business- and that means delivering on your promises and being in front of referral sources (real estate agents) constantly.

You must get people to know you before they will trust you, so stop sitting in your office wondering why business is not coming in. Get out there.

Always remember: People do business with people they like!

I am available to any inspector anytime to talk business. It is my passion.

Getting Sued

By Micheal Casey

Casey O'Malley Associates

Why do good inspectors get sued? Here at COA (Casey O'Malley Associates), we have been retained as a consultant and/or an expert in over 600 inspector related claims. We talk to a lot of inspectors who are personally disturbed by the inference that he or she did not perform per industry standard (negligence or even gross negligence), committed fraud or even worked in collusion with the agent and seller to conceal defects (yes, we've seen this allegation several times).

While it sucks to get sued; that's why there are ways to protect yourself.

Getting up every day is a risk. You risk falling in the shower or choking on your breakfast, you risk a lawsuit when you drive your vehicle and you risk a claim or suit when you do an inspection. I got sued when I was a plumbing contractor back in the 70's by a client who alleged I killed her greenhouse flowers- the judge agreed with me that it was probably the Connecticut weather. Clearly not my fault — but she believed it was or at least *wanted to believe it was my fault*.

The typical lawsuit which includes the home inspector also names the seller, the listing and selling agents, and pretty much anyone who stepped on the property during escrow or prior. Any attorney worth his or her hourly fee would be negligent not to try and get restitution from anyone possible – in particular anyone with insurance. So get used to the risk. There is risk in any profession and Home Inspection is one of the lower claims ratio professions there is. Try being a roofing contractor, attorney, or even better, a physician! These practitioners pay way more than we do for insurance than home inspectors. Yes you can be the best inspector out there, but sooner or later the numbers will result in a claim, no matter how farfetched it seems. Many claims we see are regarding items that were clearly reported. However, there is a cost to defend and attorneys know this.

Most inspectors who are sued never hear anything from the clients indicating their dissatisfaction until the summons arrives at their door. Don't take it personal; you are a target because the clients are unhappy and you might have some level of donation to be released. Don't call the attorney or client and ask why. Do contact your insurance representative and report the claim; they will handle it. If you don't have insurance - call an attorney to respond to the claim. In most states if you are incorporated an attorney must handle the claim if it's for more than $1000-$1500. But I don't want to get too far into details here. The key is getting used to some risk in any profession, in particular if you are the company principal. The other key is knowing it's not usually the cost of the repair that is big ticket- it's the cost to defend. This is why insurance is so important- you contain your risk by knowing the maximum out of pocket for a major claim is your deductible (unless you subscribe to the Inspector Services Group's 90-Day Warranty program and/or COA's Support Network wherein your deductible is likely nothing). I don't mean the occasional small claim for a minor "missed" item. In these cases you might just report it as an incident to your insurance company and negotiate a settlement yourself. Best is to just refund the fee and *always* obtain an unconditional release (not something written on the check) to dispose of the claim and the client forever.

Despite simple ways to deal with risk, many in our industry live in fear of liability and often forget that the ultimate risk is not offering service and not getting paid at all.

Winning = Answering the Phone!

By Paul Zak

America's Call Center

You want to know the difference between an inspector and an *inspection company?*

It's the impression your prospective client gets when they dial your number.

Do you answer the phone and risk annoying your client and their agent at an inspection? If you don't, the caller will move on to the next inspector on their list. If you do answer it, your client and agent may repay your rudeness with a glare and fewer or no referrals.

The caller may leave a voicemail message or may not, but in all cases they will likely move on and call the next inspector on their list. Inspectors can dance around this question all they want- there's no right answer. It doesn't matter if you quietly sneak out to your truck, or if everyone is in another room, it *is not professional* and everyone notices.

Even one missed call or one hurried call that does not impress the caller is a potential lost inspection. What is the cost of losing that job...$300, $400, $600, more? Potentially thousands when you consider future referrals?

The math is painful. Miss a call, miss an inspection job worth a lot of money, plus miss the ongoing referrals from that job. Research shows that if callers get voicemail, fifty percent of the time they will not leave a voicemail message.

If you're interested in going multi-inspector at some point you might try taking all the calls. Wise business people know they can't do everything. They know they need to find others to help.

Most of your local competition are answering their own phones and sounding like it. The way to differentiate yourself is to stand out as being more professional, more established, and of a higher caliber by having your phone professionally cared for- whether that means a full-time staff in your own office or an outsourced call center is really a matter of budget.

How much sense does it make for you, an inspector that bills your time for anywhere from $100 to $300 or even more per hour to do an administrative job worth $10 to $20 per hour?

If you're planning on being successful, you have to figure out what your "A" time is- which for you might be inspecting, it might be marketing, or it might even be training a new inspector. If your "A" time is answering the phone, you have a very basic structural problem in your business.

This is what successful inspectors do...they are there when their clients and agents need them, and they win because of it! They win with more inspections, more revenue per inspection, an enhanced professional image, and they get their life back.

You won't find an inspector in the top 5% of revenue producing home inspection companies answering their own phones- and that's not a coincidence.

One Simple Fix

By Mike Crow

Millionaire Inspector Community

When I see an inspector go hungry it bothers me – because it is easily fixed and there are just a couple of things they need to do to fix it... they need to market – properly. They need to promote- with the right message.

You need to make sure people don't choose you on price alone. I bet you deal with low price inspectors – in our market (Dallas/Fort Worth) there are people that will do inspections for $125, any size home (up to 4000 square feet), includes pier and beam foundations, swimming pool, sprinkler, and even the termite inspection. You don't want to market on price or you lose – so how do we fix this?

So, the first thing everyone thinks about is to market – but if you do it wrong (or market the wrong thing) – it won't work. Believe me, many think they already market or know how to market, but they really don't do it right.

We can look at something for a lifetime and take it for granted. I've done so on many occasions, and we're all guilty of it on some level in our businesses.

Here is a great example of this - I met a man while I was on the road. He was struggling to get inspection business, and he signed up for one of my programs. He never implemented anything, didn't join us for any of the calls, and probably never even opened our new member package when we sent it to him. Very shortly after signing up, he cancelled his membership in my coaching program. He wasn't the first, won't be the last, but then the unexpected happened...He joined again. (A friend of his in the business had joined at the same time he had originally and was doing quite well with our programs I later found out)

This time he came up to me personally at an event and asked if I would review his brochure and business card. He was much more open to new ideas and ready to take his message and market it heavily. I told him I would try at lunch and asked how his business was doing – he said lousy – and I made a commitment to get with him that day.

When we met, I reviewed his brochure and business card as he had asked and I found a fatal flaw. They looked great. The color was wonderful. He even had testimonials and had utilized both sides of his business card. He had followed almost everything I suggested in my sessions. *Almost.*

I realized he had NO USPs (Unique Selling Points). Everything he said was generic in nature – even the testimonials. When I pointed this out he asked me – "USPs? Give me an example..."

Without these you can't hope to win against the price shoppers. He had the general concept of what a USP was, it's a differentiator. He just needed some ideas for USPs that he could use.

Now I want to share with you some of the Top USPs being utilized in the industry today and what I shared with him...

- 90 Day warranties

- Discount coupons (i.e. Lowes and Home Depot)

- Reports delivered on-site

- One-stop shopping (i.e. termite, sprinkler, pool, Radon, mold)

- Uniformed inspectors

- E & O Insurance with referral protection

- Free maintenance booklet with each inspection

- RecallChek

- Free alarm inspection

- Online scheduling

- WiFi hotspot at every inspection

This was a basic list, there's dozens more where these came from, but this inspector picked up on four or five he could implement quickly and easily and add to all of his marketing materials and it worked.

The following year, his business was up over 40%. The year after that, it was up yet again an additional 30%. No other change in his business other than adding a few USPs and routinely marketing them.

You should have at least 3 USPs (Unique Selling Points) that set you apart from most of your competition and you must have at least one USP that makes you different than most all of your competition – for the record that is four USPs –

and there are more than four on the list above that cost little to nothing at all.

The more successful members of the Millionaire Inspector Community have 10+ USPs.

Of course, what's the point in being different if nobody knows? Get the word out! Tell people what makes you different when they call, brag about why you are the better home inspection company in your brochures and on your website, and just watch what happens when you go to a sales meeting or meet with an agent and say something more than the typical, "I do a really good inspection," it will change your business forever and the way customers and clients view your business forever.

Figure out what makes you unique, and if there isn't anything fix it!

Just remember— you still have to do a good solid inspection. If you aren't delivering a top notch service you will get the business once – if you are lucky twice from an agent – after that, inferior service gets what it deserves.

Be Successful and Be Around Those That Are Successful.

Streamline Your Company

By Dan Huber

Over the last 20 years the industry has evolved. Basic hand written reports, lack of inspector licensing and the limited existence of support services are no longer problems. Now the professional property inspector has access to software solutions, licensing programs and numerous support services. There is a wealth of information and resources out there to help you manage your company whether you are a single inspector, part of a multi-inspector firm or part of a national franchise system.

The question is: are you spending enough time educating yourself about what is truly available right now with today's technology?

Automation comes in an assortment of forms. It does not mean less service to your clients and agents. It simply means making more money in less time. It means being able to add another inspector to your team so you both benefit from your business model and systems.

I am a former owner of an independent inspection company with nine full-time inspectors. With automation and a complete business model utilizing the new technologies the sky is the limit. You can capture more time with your family and maintain the same amount of inspections you already perform or choose to increase volume.

Let us break down the different aspects of the inspection business and explore the idea of fine tuning your business so you can seize your share of business.

1.   Receive inspection orders as efficiently as possible:

Agents and clients should be able to order an inspection 24 hours a day on your website. Make sure your online calendar integrates with your office calendar and your mobile calendar. When someone places an order online make sure you are automatically receiving an email on your office computer or phone when an online order is placed. Next, make sure an email is automatically sent to the agent and/or client to confirm the online order. In addition, when your administrator or your call center takes an inspection order the agent and real estate office information should be available to you immediately. Look for a process which allows you to enter the information once and use it over and over again. Receiving orders should be a painless process for everyone involved.

2.   Electronic Field reports:

There are amazing electronic field reports that will save you time and improve your report presentation. If you are not up to speed on what the new reports can do for you, you owe it to yourself to see what is possible and what suits your market and style. That does not mean three minutes on a website. Ask the company for a webinar to show you what they can really do for you. The new reports of today can look and feel completely different with a few clicks. Check boxes, narratives or a blend are possible from the same report system. If you are using a paper report you are losing market share to your competitors. If you are using an old electronic report without great technical support now is the time to upgrade. If you have not reviewed the top 4 or 5 software companies in the last 12 months you may not know what you are missing. All the information taken on your order form should auto populate into your electronic report. Do not spend your valuable time with unnecessary typing.

3.   Send out agreements, invoices and reports automatically.

You really should automate the delivery of your agreements, invoices and reports. Make sure you can send them out with a few short "clicks" with no need for additional typing. You want to deliver a great presentation every time in the same manner: ready to print or be emailed in an instant.

4.   Your schedule should be prepared for you including maps and drive time:

Make sure your daily schedule overview is delivered to you in an automated fashion. The perfect example: receive an email with your inspections for the next day including all the details you need and a driving map. You do not need an assistant, family member, or worse, yourself to do these tasks when you can automate it!

5.   Automate confirmation and 24 hour reminder emails:

Your automated system should send out confirmation emails and SMS/texts to the agents and client. How about

24 hours before the inspection send another email and or SMS/text to remind them of the inspection and remind them about the utilities being turned on? Email and SMS/text automation should be customizable and limited only by your imagination.

6.   Are you a tracker?:

No, I do not mean deer or moose.

With today's automation you must have information gathered for you that will assist you in decisions about running your company. How many inspections has Bill Agent done with you this year? How about his RE/MAX™ Company? How many inspections have you done in a particular zip code or town? How many Radon (or other environmental) inspections did you do versus regular residential inspections? What is your average inspection fee amount? Did you know today is Jill Agent's birthday? If you are properly automated all these statistics will be at your fingertips. With this kind of powerful data you can shape your company to be all it can be.

Can you go to one screen on your computer and see a complete timeline of any inspection? It is powerful on many fronts to quickly view when the order was taken. When the agreement was sent and signed. This not only reduces your potential liability but will help you effectively answer any questions from agents and clients in a positive and professional manner. You should not have to do any of this manually. Not only is this great information to have available for running your day–to-day operation but could help reduce your liability in litigation.

7.   Are you using a system that protects your data?:

Storing reports and business documents in your office or garage is a problem waiting to happen. Online storage allows you to access your information from any internet connection in the world. No more digging through boxes for an old report or worrying about a fire, flood or where to build more shelves. Protect yourself by placing your information in a safe environment. A terrible scenario to recognize: if your office burned to the ground could you go to work tomorrow? Where is your calendar? How about your hard drive backup? Did you really back-up your laptop last month? All of these terrible scenarios are avoided with high-quality automated and protected systems.

8.   Are you using technology to offer other services to your clients to be more of service and make more money?

Offering extra services such as discounts on alarm systems, RecallChek, "We have moved labels" and postcards and more are important parts of today's inspection marketing platforms.

Whether you are just getting started in the business or have been inspecting for years, I hope you make the best of the tools available today. Automation will save you time and create better relationships which will equate to more money in your pocket.

Spending some time to truly see what is possible is the key.

You Should Have Multiple Websites

By Dominic Maricic

When I first started giving talks on website optimization, marketing and social networking in 2008 less than 20% the room had a website. Today, over 90% have a website. So my first goal of making sure every inspector has a website is almost complete. Now it's time to spread the word of the next goal for home inspectors...having more than one website!

 If you've heard my talk before you've heard me mention many times that your site needs to be targeted to at most 5 specific keyword search phrases, revolving around 'city name home inspector.' Many of you have expressed the great difficulty in choosing JUST 5 names. But if you ask any of the people who have listened to me and limited the focus of their site, you will hear them tell you that they rank towards the top of the search engine in those cities. Inspectors that have listened and implemented what I talk about, many of whom also host their sites with us have the top sites in almost every major city in the country. I've worked with thousands of inspectors on their websites. Those that work the hardest have gone from 0 inspections a month from their website to 30 or more inspections a month directly through their site (the top inspector I've seen was able to document over 60 inspections a month through his site found through search engines).

So, why get more than one website? To get to the top of the search engines you have to convince the search engine that your site is the most relevant site for that city. The best way to do this is to focus on one area or service throughout each site. If your site is only about being a home inspector in Chicago then the search engines will clearly know what your site is about and raise its rank on the search engines.

Can you target more than one city on each site? The answer is, "It depends." If you're in a more rural area, the answer is yes. If you are in a densely populated area and there are tons of inspectors in the area then you need to concentrate that site on one specific city to get to the top of the search engines faster.

The other important thing to remember is that you can't use the exact same content on all the websites or Google (the main search engine) is going to look at your site and determine that you're a copycat and lower your site rank. Your content can be similar, just don't copy and paste it all. Use those high school skills of rewriting things you found in a book to avoid plagiarism (your English teacher told you they would pay off!).

Multiple sites doesn't stop with focusing on different inspection sites for different cities. It also extends to different ancillary services that you offer. If you offer services like mold, radon, and pest inspections and you want to be #1 on Google when someone searches for a mold inspector in your site, create a separate site focused on mold inspections.

All this may seem like a lot of work for those of you getting started on your first site but you'll find that the task actually gets a lot easier after you finish a site. More importantly, once your business starts to take off due to your website, you'll be driven to work on more sites to increase your business even more!

Buying multiple domains at once? Save some money by going to www.economicaldomains.com.

The Rising Tide

By Hollis Brown

YadZooks

Home Inspectors gain from their competitors' successes to some extent, whether they realize it or not.

Most inspectors don't market themselves in a way that harms competing inspectors in the first place, which may seem counterintuitive to marketing experts in other industries. Home inspection isn't a zero sum game- it's an expanding marketplace.

Consider the state of the profession in the early 1980's when few homes sold were inspected. Inspectors across the country found very real benefit in banding together into organizations that built credibility of the home inspection process and the inspectors who provided the service. This important gust of credibility put wind in the sails of many of the skiffs that home inspection professionals were launching across the country. As word got out that a home inspection could help a home buyer avoid unpleasant surprises after settlement, demand for home inspections grew- and as much as some in our industry might not believe it, this came mostly from real estate agents wanting to protect their clients. Credibility was key. Strict adherence to standards of practice and codes of ethics kept the reputation of home inspectors positive. We home inspectors owe considerable debt to the pioneers who fostered good will with the entire real estate community.

Today, the real estate community is the reason that most all owner occupied resale homes get home inspections. The inspection is mentioned in the purchase contract, and most agents have a referral list that might have three inspectors on it- it might only have one and I hope that is you.

At this point, where there is so much business out there and real estate transaction inspections are so commonplace, we need to be reminded that there are two ways that business is generated—conversion and creation.

Some competitors strive to convert. They enter the market place with their eye on the business that the competition is doing and devise a marketing strategy designed to reconfigure the stream of business from other businesses to their own. They adjust their prices. They put on sales and promote featured products. Let's call them Converters.

The home inspection profession was launched on the premise that, "All older homes should be inspected." The inspection focused on age within the context of life expectancy, damage and deterioration. Converters worked diligently to capture market share.

Other competitors, however, suggested that new homes should be inspected too. Let's call them innovators.

Innovators went after the 11-month inspections for new construction homes before the walk through with their builder.

Innovators created the multi-stage new construction inspection.

Innovators added services like pool inspections and sprinkler systems.

Where will the next innovation be?

I encourage you to participate in that discussion and it's happening right now in online groups on Facebook and LinkedIn. It's happening on forums like Brian Hannigan's and it's happening on the InterNACHI forum as well.

The power of all this is yet to be realized and I'm excited about the future.

Chapter 17
Resources

There are skills needed for doing your job- and sometimes certifications required for offering various services. *Don't mistake being able to perform a task with being able to make money doing it.*

You'll find in this section the leading vendors in the home inspection industry, and every single one has something you should add to your marketing toolbox and implement immediately. The only thing to gain by waiting is lost revenue and lost opportunity.

Software

Software should make your job easy, allow you to brand yourself well, and integrate with the services you need to grow your business. No one was offered the opportunity to pay to be on this list of the best software in the inspection industry- they were handpicked. All of them have the support staff necessary to fulfill your needs, the programming wherewithal to make changes as needed, and all have shown the ability and willingness to support their users through integration with third parties. Each of the software companies listed has either already integrated with RecallChek for instance (or has made a programming commitment to do so), and many of them integrate with each other. For instance, a 3-D report can be uploaded to the Schedule Center with ease and an appointment made in the Inspection Support Network can automatically download into the Home Inspector Pro template. Systems and processes like these not only make your job easier, it also allows for easy expansion when it's time to hire more home inspectors.

All of these providers share the philosophy that the home inspector's brand comes first. You won't find them directing traffic of your agents and clients to their site- it's YOUR client and it's YOUR brand!

The BAM Dashboard works well to supplement all of your software in promoting your company in real estate offices.

Software

3-D Inspection System
Carl Fowler
www.3dinspection.com
800-745-6126

Home Inspector Pro
Dominic Maricic
www.homeinspectorpro.com

 Inspection**Support**Network

Inspection Support Network
Dan Huber
www.inspectionsupport.net
800-700-8112

Software

 | **INSPECTOR SERVICES GROUP**

BAM (Broker/Agent Marketing) Dashboard
Inspector Services Group
Mike Doerr
www.inspectorservicesgroup.com
800-544-8156

Inspection Management Systems
Russ Colliau
www.theschedulecenter.com
800-939-9252

Carson Dunlop
John Kwasnik
www.carsondunlop.com
800-268-7070

Software

eInspections
Dan Huber
www.einspections.net
800-700-8112

Summit Systems
Barry Prentice
www.summitinspection.net

USPs (Unique Selling Propositions)

Setting yourself apart from the competition takes more than being a "good inspector." Find three or more things that you can offer that others can't or won't. Will you take my call after the inspection is complete? Really? ANYBODY can say that. Don't get me wrong, you should offer great customer service if you plan on being in business for long and it goes without saying that delivering a good, solid inspection is necessary in any inspection business.

Try this one on for size; "With every full home inspection, we offer a 90-Day Warranty that covers many things that could break shortly after you move in even if they were working fine at the time of inspection." Or maybe this one; "At the time of our inspection, we take down the make and model number of all your major appliances and check to see if any have been recalled due to fire or safety issues. It's one of many ways we provide premium service that our competition just can't keep up with."

Offering color photographs and emailed reports isn't unique anymore- it's required. The following vendors provide awesome services that your clients are going to love...but don't stop here! Come up with something uniquely your own to add to your business model.

USPs

RecallChek
P. Nathan Thornberry & Mike Doerr
www.recallchek.com
800-544-8156

**My Engineer
On Call, LLC.**

My Engineer On Call
Jeff Donaldson
www.myengineeroncall.com
866-743-6448

Radalink (Radon Monitors with the *Radon Protection Plan*-the
ultimate USP for your Radon testing business)
Terry Howell
www.radalink.com
800-295-4655

USPs

90-Day Warranties from Residential Warranty Services
The Inspector Services Group
P. Nathan Thornberry & Mike Doerr
www.90daywarranty.com
800-544-8156

TERMITE
PROTECTION PLAN

The Inspector Services Group Termite Protection Plan
P. Nathan Thornberry & Mike Doerr
www.inspectorservicesgroup.com
800-544-8156

Alarm Inspection Certification
Bill Gustafson
www.alarminspection.com
800-544-8156

USPs

INSPECTOR SERVICES GROUP

The Alarm Leads Program
Inspector Services Group
P. Nathan Thornberry & Bill Gustafson
www.alarmleadsprogram.com
800-544-8156

*The Alarm Leads Program not only allows for the USP of offering clients a discount on alarm monitoring, it offers a compliant way to receive some of the other products listed in this section for free or even receive cash.

203k in a box
Catherine Hall
www.203kinabox.com

There are many ways to become a 203k inspector, I prefer to let Catherine do the work in getting me there!

Insurance (Errors & Omissions)

In the constantly evolving world of real estate and home inspection, it's important to protect yourself from liability. That means doing a good inspection, responding to complaints diligently, and having an insurance policy for when things go wrong.

Insurance has become a marketing edge as well- especially policies with referral protection for agents.

Rates and programs change constantly. Insurance programs have come and gone. These providers, starting with Bob Pearson of Allen Insurance, have shown the ability to not only stay in business but also the ability to help inspectors reduce their claims.

They also happen to have a deductible that is pretty close to the limit of the E & O Deductible Protection users of certain Inspector Services Group products receive. In other words, talk to one of these insurance agents, then talk to the Inspector Services Group, and you'll have a $0.00 deductible.

It's not only cool, it's just plain smart business.

Insurance

Allen Insurance
group

Allen Insurance Group
Bob Pearson
www.allenins.com
800-474-4472

FREA
Ben Garrison
www.FREA.com
800-882-4410

InspectorPro Insurance Program
Will Colton
www.inspectorproinsurance.com
866-916-9420

Insurance

Elite InspectInsure
Teresa Murray
www.eiipro.com
800-355-1185

For a complete list of home inspection errors & omissions insurance providers, contact the Inspector Services Group at 800-544-8156.

Call Centers

Missing a call is expensive. If you don't think that's the case, you're lying to yourself. If you do the math properly, you'll find that you need at least three and possibly as many as five inspectors before hiring an office person makes sense financially...and even then you can only take one call at a time!

If you want to be successful, go where successful inspectors go- and they're decidedly split between two concepts.

One concept would be part-time and backup call answering- a service offered by the Inspector Services Group Call Center exclusively for home inspectors. This program allows inspectors to answer the phone when they're available and not pay someone else to take an order when they were available to do so themselves.

The other concept is full-time "office management," offered by America's Call Center (also exclusively for home inspectors). Paul Zak takes a more personal approach to the business- he wants to handle every call he can for you and make your life easy. It costs a bit more than the part-time services offered by the Inspector Services Group, but the return on that investment in terms of consistency and sanity is pretty good.

Call Centers

**The Leader in Scheduling and
Phone Answering Services
Exclusively for Home Inspectors**

America's Call Center
Paul Zak
www.americascallcenter.com
888-462-6153

 | **INSPECTOR SERVICES GROUP**

The Call Center
Inspector Services Group
Nick Bates
www.inspectorservicesgroup.com
800-544-8156

Connections

Everyone likes to be connected. No one likes to be an outsider.

If you have ever walked into a room and it seemed that a group of people on the other side of the room were talking about you- it likely stirred one of two things in your mind;

1. *Feeling like you might not be well liked or your fly is unzipped or something.*

2. *Thinking to yourself, "Of course they're talking about me, I'm famous!"*

Well, I always go with number two, and you will as well once you're on the inside!

This section is for strictly those things that the top inspectors in the country have in common. MOST inspectors have a connection to one of these things, all successful inspectors have a connection with most or all of them.

It's boarding time...will you get upgraded to first class? It's up to you...

Connections

HomeInspectorWebinar.com

Operated by...
P. Nathan Thornberry, Mike Doerr, & Bill Gustafson

The Inspector Services Group holds webinars regularly on marketing topics that most inspectors aren't interested in, and few will grasp. Every single one is designed to get you thinking...not to necessarily take the information and use it. Over 500 inspectors from all across the U.S. and Canada stumble in about once every month after the kids are asleep to plan world domination. It's a lot of fun...and NOT for the timid.

www.CaseyOMalleyAssociates.com
www.HomeInspectorSupport.com
www.InspectionConference.com

Casey O'Malley Associates
Michael Casey & Kevin O'Malley
www.inspectionconference.com
www.homeinspectorsupport.com
866-363-1330

Legendary inspection conferences and one of the most innovative services ever- the COA Support Network. Get inspection questions answered live via their application while you're at the property. Awesome.

Connections

Yadzooks
Hollis Brown
www.YadZooks.com

If you're in the home inspection business and you're not listed on this site, you better check your watch because you're running way behind.

Millionaire Inspector Community
Mike Crow
www.mikecrow.com

If you haven't heard Mike Crow speak at least once, you've missed out on decades of experience from a second generation inspector that built and sold one inspection company, and is working on his next. Fast-forward your experience level by ten years...even if you've been in it for thirty.

*Get in touch with either Mike Crow or Mike Doerr regarding pricing structure for multi-inspector firms as referenced in Chapter 14: *The Multi-Inspector Mindset.*

Connections

One-on-One w/Mike Doerr!
Mike Doerr
800-544-8156

Mike Doerr is famous for his One-on-One consultations with home inspection companies big and small. There's no qualification for talking to him, you don't have to be a client or pay anything- but it will change everything.

Did I mention it was free?

Joe Ferry, Claim Intercept
www.joeferry.com

You've never met an attorney that understands what we do the way Joe does. Take a look at his Claim Intercept service and keep it in your back pocket for when you bump into the right mental patient.

Connections

Home Inspector Pro- Web Hosting & Web Classes
Dominic Maricic
www.homeinspectorpro.com

Anybody who's anybody has heard Dominic talk about optimization of home inspector websites. Find out where he's going to be, go there. If you have a website already, and you're in love with it, great. If you want a website that works for your business, talk to Dominic and then look at his web hosting options.

TOP (Total Online Presence) Marketing
Inspector Services Group
800-544-8156

If you've seen an inspector with an awesome video on their website, or a Facebook page with more than 100 fans and a cool custom application...it's NOT something they just figured out on their own. It's a system that makes you look like a professional enterprise, it's cheap, and it's guaranteed. It works.

Associations

InterNACHI has some amazing resources. Both ASHI and NAHI have created a national reputation for quality. Local organizations such as CREIA, FABI, and many others have worked hard at establishing local connections with real estate organizations.

None of these associations have heavy fees or make it difficult to join- and my rule is belong to any that matter to your business.

If there are agents in your area that tell their clients to ask if you belong to a particular organization, join it. If you are looking for some support you're not getting at one organization, join another. It's cheap.

Better yet, go to a conference or two every year, and seek out business opportunities as well as educational credits. The most successful home inspectors I know attend conferences regularly.

Join your local association, but consider joining at least one, if not all three of the following nationwide associations (and CAHPI in Canada).

Associations (in no particular order)

American Society of Home Inspectors
www.ASHI.org

International Association of Certified Home Inspectors
www.interNACHI.org

NATIONAL ASSOCIATION OF
HOME INSPECTORS, INC.
National Association of Home Inspectors
www.NAHI.org

Franchise Systems

I've had the pleasure of working with many of the franchise systems in the home inspection industry, and franchisees from literally all of them.

Resources you can get from vendors like myself can oftentimes be purchased in bulk through a franchise system- and much of the hassle of creating marketing materials and arranging for things like backup call centers is done for you in many cases as part of your franchisor's offering.

In other words, there's a lot to consider beyond the simple cost of obtaining a franchise territory and the ongoing franchise fees.

Just like going at it alone isn't something I would encourage, a franchise isn't for everyone either- but if you were considering a franchise opportunity, this is a list of the leading franchises in the business. All of them offer phenomenal resources.

Franchise Systems (in no particular order)

HouseMaster
www.housemaster.com

Pillar to Post
www.pillartopost.com

HomeTeam
www.hometeaminspection.com

WIN
www.wini.com

Amerispec
www.amerispec.com

Franchise Systems (in no particular order)

The Brickkicker
www.brickkicker.com

Inspect-It 1st
www.inspectit1st.com

NPI/GPI
www.npiweb.com

1st Inspection Services
www.1stinspections.com

The Hungry Home Inspector

By P. Nathan Thornberry
The Inspector Services Group
All Rights Reserved
2012